POETRY OF THE FIRST WORLD WAR

EDITED BY AND WITH AN
INTRODUCTION
BY MARCUS CLAPHAM

Collector's Library

First published in 2013 by Collector's Library
an imprint of Pan Macmillan
20 New Wharf Road, London N1 9RR
Associated companies throughout the world
www.panmacmillan.com

ISBN 978-1-9096-2100-8

3

A CIP catalogue record for this book is available from the British Library.

Typeset by Bookcraft Ltd
Printed and bound in China by Imago

Visit **www.panmacmillan.com** to read more about all our books
and to buy them. You will also find features, author interviews and
news of any author events, and you can sign up for e-newsletters
so that you're always first to hear about our new releases.

INTRODUCTION

Adlestrop

Yes. I remember Adlestrop
The name, because one afternoon
Of heat, the express-train drew up there
Unwontedly. It was late June.

The steam hissed. Someone cleared his throat.
No one left and no one came
On the bare platform. What I saw
Was Adlestrop—only the name

And willows, willow-herb, and grass,
And meadowsweet, and haycocks dry,
No whit less still and lonely fair
Than the high cloudlets in the sky.

And for that minute a blackbird sang
Close by, and round him, mistier,
Farther and farther, all the birds
Of Oxfordshire and Gloucestershire

This poem describes an incident in Edward Thomas's journey to Dymock on 24th June 1914, four days before the assassination of Archduke Franz Ferdinand of Austria in Sarajevo, which set in train the events which led to the outbreak of what came to be known as The Great War. Written in January 1915 before Thomas enlisted, it seems to encapsulate the prelapsarian ideal of the endless Edwardian summer. It was for this ideal that young men answered Lord Kitchener's 'Your Country Needs You' by volunteering for the New

Armies in tens of thousand for an adventure that was widely thought would be over by Christmas. They lost their illusions in the gas at Loos and on the uncut barbed wire of the Somme.

The poetry of the First World War is remarkable in its endurance, its quantity and above all its power to animate an episode in human history we should never allow ourselves to forget. It is strange that poetry written in such appalling conditions a hundred years ago should still have the ability to move its readers and those who hear it read. It produces in the reader or hearer an astonished pity for the waste of men and the suffering that they endured in the first protracted industrialised conflict since the American Civil War fifty years previously. In the much-quoted phrase from Wilfred Owen's Preface 'My subject is War and the pity of War. The Poetry is in the pity.' He goes on to say 'Yet these elegies are to this generation in no sense consolatory. They may be to the next. All a poet can do today is warn. That is why the true Poets must be truthful.' His poems are, to some extent, consolatory to succeeding generations, but the warning is perhaps even stronger.

There are nearly seventy poets in this anthology, and they represent only a very small proportion of those who wrote about the war. Poets whose subject was war came from all backgrounds, because the great Victorian educational reforms had produced a remarkably literate population and, in an age when the cinema was in its infancy, entertainment consisted largely of reading and music. Recitations at home, in public houses and music halls were immensely popular, and the balladic rhythms of poets such as Rudyard Kipling, Robert W. Service, George Leybourne, Albert Chevalier and J. Milton Hayes were well known.

The anonymous pieces at the beginning of the book give a small indication of the sardonic parodies that combine church and music hall antecedents, and date from the middle of the war. In its early days, a romantic optimism informed the patriotic verse of 1914:

'Now God be thanked'

wrote the golden-haired Rupert Brooke

'Who hath matched us with His hour
And caught our youth, and wakened us
   from sleeping.'

For many, the Edwardian and early Georgian eras were ones of tawdry values in which scandal and hypocrisy in public life abounded, and labour unrest, Suffragettes and Irish Home Rule dominated domestic politics. Popular perception of warfare envisaged a war of movement, of cavalry charges and horse artillery, founded largely on memories of the Second Boer War. As far as war in Europe was concerned, longer memories harked back to the Franco-Prussian War of 1870 which was over in a matter of months. When war broke out in August 1914, the generally accepted view in Britain was that it would be over quickly. Thousands of young men of all classes enlisted at once, keen to escape the *ennui* of their workaday lives, and see some action before the war ended.

Hindsight is wonderfully clear, and it is easy to see the unfolding of events following the assassination of Franz Ferdinand as a Greek tragedy. The Austrians declared war on Serbia, the Russians mobilised in support of Serbia, the Germans mobilised in support of Austria, the French mobilised in support of Russia and Great Britain and its Empire mobilised when the Germans invaded Belgium. The famous Schlieffen Plan, which might have ended the war by Christmas, was so adapted by German caution that Joffre, with some help from the British Expeditionary Force, was able to halt the German advance. Then followed the sportily named 'race for the sea' in which opposing forces dug trench fortifications from the North Sea to the Swiss border. It was these trenches that inspired most of the poems in this book.

Trench life was hellish for all sides, especially for the British (though the French army endured its own Calvary of Verdun). They held the line from near the Belgian coast in the north to the Somme in the south. Along the whole line the Germans tended to hold the high ground. Not only that, but the incessant use of high-explosive shells destroyed the drainage system of the Flemish Plain so that British trenches were frequently waterlogged, giving rise to many health problems, and it was little better further south in Picardy. The German imperative in this stalemate was not to be defeated, while the Allies' prime concern was to win and recapture lost territories, entailing what was effectively siege warfare. Although heavy artillery bombardment was the main attacking arm, when it had done what work it could against enemy

6

batteries, machine-gun nests, pill-boxes and barbed wire, it was the front-line soldier who had to try to occupy enemy territory. This exposed him to death by rifle fire, mortar fire, machine-gun fire, gas, and the possibility of obliteration or dismemberment from a direct hit by a shell. If he reached the enemy front line, hand-grenades, side-arms and bayonets still awaited him. Merely occupying the front line was fraught with danger – from artillery and mortar shells which could bury dozens, from snipers and from health hazards such as trench fever, which was caused by the ubiquitous lice and nits, and trench foot caused by prolonged exposure of the feet to damp, unsanitary and cold conditions, which were common in the early stages of the war, having trench foot was a punishable offence, as was venereal disease throughout the war; there were many ludicrous regulations that had to be borne as well – see Wilfred Owen's 'Inspection' – and officially the upper lip might not be shaved. With the arrival of Kitchener's New Armies, which contained young men who were incapable of growing moustaches, this regulation was abolished by an Army Order dated 6 October 1916 issued by Lieutenant-General Sir Nevil Macready, Adjutant-General to the Forces (who loathed his own moustache and immediately shaved it off). Even out of the line, in support, in reserve or resting, soldiers were not necessarily safe from enemy action, and the din of gunfire was always with them.

In or out of the line, soldiers lived in a mad and terrible world of their own. The desolation and ruin of the country in which they fought was almost unimaginable. (Perhaps the two most telling descriptions are by novelists who never fought in the trenches. The end of Evelyn Waugh's *Vile Bodies* has a description of a ruined battlefield that is memorably ghastly, and Sebastian Faulks's *Birdsong* sustains the banal horror of everyday life in and below the trench systems.) The daily routine of life at the front was a mixture of squalor and boredom, punctuated by moments of terror. Food was generally brought up to the line in dixies (large iron cooking pots) and was likely to be cold on arrival. Water was carried up in cans that had been used for petrol, and tasted of it. Latrines were primitive and disgusting, not infrequently hit by shell or mortar fire. The stench of nearby latrines, unwashed bodies and the putrefying remains of men and horses would have been horrific, though front-line soldiers could become so accustomed to the smell that they no longer noticed it. And then there were the rats. They were huge, some, reputedly, growing to the size of cats, and one pair could produce 800 offspring in a year. They fed on discarded rations, the remains in food cans and, most disconcertingly, on the bodies of unburied soldiers in no-man's-land and in the trenches themselves. They infested the dugouts and crawled over the faces of sleeping men. One veteran claimed that if you stood still for long enough, they would eat the leather laces of your boots.

Life out of the line was hardly comfortable either. Billets were primitive, bathing and de-lousing humiliating, and the clean clothes might well have lice eggs in the seams which the body heat of the wearer would hatch. Entertainment was frequently limited to cheap wine and egg and chips at a local *estaminet,* but for those troops stationed near the larger towns such as Amiens or Albert, better food was available in restaurants and cafés, and the existence of blue lamp brothels for officers and red lamp brothels for other ranks was tolerated on the grounds that they were good for morale.

This prurient detail is not irrelevant to the poetry of the First World War. Although British troops on the Western Front were fighting so close to south-east England that barrages and detonation of mines could be heard by the Prime Minister in Downing Street, they lived in an alien world far apart from the wildest imaginings of those at home. Because of this, many troops – though we have mainly officers' accounts – were alienated from their friends and family on the Home Front. It was impossible to discuss or even describe the realities of modern war. By 1915 the high-flown language of the early days was not in general use at the Front. Perhaps the most famous poem of the war, 'In Flanders Fields' by John McCrae displays a fatalism in the first two verses but, by the last one, has reverted to the 'noble' sentiments expected of 'heroes'. It was written in November 1915 at a time when the old military certainties were being challenged as Douglas Haig replaced Sir John French as Commander-in-Chief. In the poem found in Charles Sorley's kit after he was killed at the Battle of Loos in October 1915, 'When You See Millions of the Mouthless Dead', this resignation is even more marked, and is a long way from his pastoral verse of only a year earlier.

From early 1916 onwards, after the 1915 calamities of the Second Battle of Ypres in April, Loos and the Dardanelles, a hopeless fatalism set in among fighting men and officers. While at the Front many may have wished for a 'Blighty' wound that would have them sent home, having spent time with uncomprehending family and friends they frequently wanted to return to the companions in their units with whom they had something in common. Jerome Kern's 'They Didn't Believe Me' was adapted as:

And when they ask us, how dangerous it was,
Oh, we'll never tell them, no, we'll never tell them:
We spent our pay in some cafe,
And fought wild women night and day,
'Twas the cushiest job we ever had.
And when they ask us, and they're certainly
    going to ask us,
The reason why we didn't win the Croix de Guerre,
Oh, we'll never tell them, oh, we'll never tell them
There was a front, but damned if we knew where.

Another cynical adaptation that expressed the common youthful feeling of immortality went:

The bells of hell go ting-a-ling-a-ling
For you but not for me:
And the little devils how they sing-a-ling-a-ling
For you but not for me.
O death, where is thy sting-a-ling-a-ling,
O grave, thy victory?
The bells of hell go ting-a-ling-a-ling,
For you but not for me.

By 1916, this alienation was beginning to appear in verse. Sassoon's vicious 'They' and 'Base Details' were followed the next year by the equally harsh 'The General', 'Does It Matter' and 'To Any Dead Officer'. 1917 was the year of Sassoon's 'Soldier's Declaration' of his opposition to the war and his subsequent time at Craiglockhart War Hospital, where he met and advised Wilfred Owen on his poetry.

Given this alienation and the inability to discuss the reality of war with those they loved, it is perhaps not surprising that soldiers looked inward, and expressed themselves in verse. Poetry, for many, became a way of articulating the fear, disgust, horror, pity, frustration and bleak hopelessness, and included bitter condemnation of the war, the military mind, war-profiteers and domestic ignorance. At other times a grim, black humour took over, as in Philip Johnstone's 'High Wood', while Hardy's pre-war 'Channel Firing' is a prescient warning of the folly that allowed the war to develop. Edward Thomas, who enlisted voluntarily at an age which could have excused his service, did not start writing poetry until shortly before the outbreak of war, and none of his poems are specifically 'war' poems. But 'As the Team's Head-Brass', 'In Memoriam', 'Lights Out' and 'The Owl' are imbued with an aching regret that is more poignant than some of the more full-on war poems.

On a lighter note we should perhaps remember A. P. Herbert's wonderful ditty. Sub-Lieutenant Herbert was a member of the Royal Naval Division, an infantry division which consisted of naval reservists and volunteers who were not required to serve at sea.

They had their own nautical traditions of discipline, which infuriated their new commander, General Hamilton Shute, when he was appointed in October 1916. Herbert wrote:

The General inspecting the trenches
Exclaimed with a horrified shout
'I refuse to command a division
Which leaves its excreta about.'

But nobody took any notice
No one was prepared to refute,
That the presence of shit was congenial
Compared to the presence of Shute.

And certain responsible critics
Made haste to reply to his words
Observing that his staff advisors
Consisted entirely of turds.

For shit may be shot at odd corners
And paper supplied there to suit,
But a shit would be shot without mourners
If somebody shot that shit Shute.

As John Bourne notes in *Who's Who in World War I*, it effectively finished him as Commander of the RND, and in February 1917 he was transferred in to the 32nd Division which he commanded with great skill and imagination.

This anthology provides only a taste of the wide variety of poetry produced during the First World War. Its aim is to introduce the reader to that variety and to encourage further reading of the many poets represented here. Some wrote very little; many were killed or died before they could develop their work. Sassoon and Owen are the giants of the English-speaking poets of the First World War, followed closely by Isaac Rosenberg and Edward Thomas. Sassoon's poetry expressed the fierce anger of the poet as a fighting man, while Owen moved beyond anger to a deep compassion. In the aftermath of war many wanted to forget the brutal realities; W.B. Yeats excluded Owen (and Sassoon, Rosenberg and Blunden) from *The Oxford Book of Modern Verse* on the grounds that 'passive suffering is not a theme for poetry' and said of Owen's poetry 'When I excluded Wilfred Owen, whom I consider unworthy of the poets' corner of a country newspaper, I did not know I was excluding a revered sandwich-board man of the revolution & that some body has put his worst & most famous poem in a glass-case in the British Museum – however if I had known it I would have excluded him just the same. He is all blood, dirt & sucked sugar stick.'

In 'On Passing the New Menin Gate' Siegfried Sassoon furiously asked:

Who will remember, passing through this Gate
The unheroic dead who fed the guns?
Who shall absolve the foulness of their fate –
Those doomed, conscripted, unvictorious ones?

We may not now absolve their fate, but thanks to the poetry of the soldiers who fought alongside them, we will remember them.

BIBLIOGRAPHY
POETS AND POETRY

Brian Gardner, *Up the Line to Death*, Methuen, 1964.

Vivien Noakes, *Voices of Silence*, Sutton, 2006.

Ian Parsons, *Men Who March Away*, Chatto & Windus, 1965.

Anne Powell, *A Deep Cry*, Palladour Books, 1993.

David Roberts, *We Are The Dead*, Red Horse Press, 2012.

Martin Stephen, *The Price of Pity*, Pen & Sword, 1996.

George Walter, *The Penguin Book of First World War Poetry*, Penguin, 2004.

PROSE WORKS

Edmund Blunden, *Undertones of War*, Cobden-Sanderson, 1928.

Max Egremont, *Siegfried Sassoon: A Biography*, Picador, 2005.

Paul Fussell, *The Great War and Modern Memory*, Oxford University Press, 2000.

Robert Graves, *Goodbye to All That*, Collector's Library, 2013.

A.P. Herbert, *The Secret Battle*, Methuen, 1919.

Matthew Hollis, *Now All Roads Lead to France*, Faber & Faber, 2011.

Siegfried Sassoon, *Memoirs of an Infantry Officer*, Faber & Faber, 1930.

Jon Stallworthy, *Wilfred Owen*, Oxford University Press, 1974.

POETRY OF THE
FIRST WORLD WAR

Anonymous

Après la Guerre Finie

Après la guerre finie,
Soldat anglais parti;
Mam'selle Fransay boko pleuray
Après la guerre finie.

Après la guerre finie,
Soldat anglais parti;
Mademoiselle in the family way,
Après la guerre finie,

Après la guerre finie,
Soldat anglais parti;
Mademoiselle can go to hell
Après la guerre finie.

Anonymous

I Don't Want to be a Soldier

> To the tune of 'On Sunday
> I walk out with a Soldier'

I don't want to be a soldier,
I don't want to go to war.
I'd rather stay at home,
Around the streets to roam,
And live on the earnings of a well-paid whore.
I don't want a bayonet up my arse-hole,
I don't want my ballocks shot away.
I'd rather stay in England,
In merry merry England,
And fornicate my bloody life away.

Anonymous

If You Want to Find the Sergeant

If you want to find the Sergeant,
I know where he is, I know where he is,
   I know where *he* is.
If you want to find the Sergeant
   I know where he is –
He's lying on the Canteen floor.
I've seen him, I've *seen* him,
Lying on the Canteen floor.

     *   *   *

If you want to find the old battalion,
I know where they are, I know where they are,
   I know where *they* are.
If you want to find the old battalion,
   I know where they are –
They're hanging on the old barbed wire.
I've seen 'em, I've *seen* 'em,
Hanging on the old barbed wire.

Anonymous

We are Fred Karno's Army

We are Fred Karno's army, we are the ragtime
    infantry.
We cannot fight, we cannot shoot, what bleeding use
    are we?

And when we get to Berlin we'll hear the Kaiser say,
'Hoch! Hoch! Mein Gott, what a bloody rotten lot
    are the ragtime infantry.'

Anonymous

When this Bloody War is Over

When this bloody war is over,
No more soldiering for me.
When I get my civvy clothes on,
Oh, how happy I shall be!
No more church parades on Sunday,
No more begging for a pass.
You can tell the Sergeant-Major
To stick his passes up his arse.

When this bloody war is over,
No more soldiering for me.
When I get my civvy clothes on,
Oh, how happy I shall be!
No more NCOs to curse me,
No more rotten army stew.
You can tell the old Cook-Sergeant,
To stick his stew right up his flue.

When this bloody war is over,
No more soldiering for me.
When I get my civvy clothes on,
Oh, how happy I shall be!
No more sergeants bawling
'Pick it up' and 'Put it down.'
If I meet the ugly bastard
I'll kick his arse all over town.

Raymond Asquith

Liquid Fire and Poison Gas

Liquid fire and poison gas
Leave the German where he was.
Obviously, if we can,
We must find a bolder plan.
Why not then invoke the Muse?
Surely conscience bids us use
(Since we're fighting for the Right)
Every form of Schrecklichkeit.
Then, I ask you, why not try
The magic power of poesy?
After all the thing's been done;
Goethe was a bloody Hun.
Why not in the last resort
Versify the Train Report?
I know it's going rather far,
But – anything to win the war.
Only insignificant
Traffic passed from Bruges to Ghent;
But the line from Ghent to Bruges
Is quite another pair of shoes.
Masses of marines (with guns)
Suspiciously resembling Huns
(So an agent we employ
Says – a 'personne digne de foi')
40 trains of infantry
Clothed in grey (surprisingly),
90 wagons, men or horses;
– (So we learn from other sources) –
Men or horses, Wallinger?

'Non-éclairés' probably;
But, Oh the difference to me!
Kitchens and pontoons galore –
Looks uncommon like a corps –
Bless me, what can this portend?
Are they going to Ostend?
No, they merely use this line
To conceal their real design.
They are moving troops from Ghent
To the Ypres Salient,
And I haven't any doubt
We shall trace them to Thourout
And (when the returns come in)
Very likely to Menin.
The reports from Gemmenich
Are fit to make a fellow sick
'Fantassins, Artillerie
Graviers, Pierrerie'
By this line they seem to bring
Every kind of bloody thing.
Welkenraedt is just as bad:
Details always drive me mad.
Luckily for all our sakes
Nothing ever comes through Aix.
What is this I find at Diest?
Quite an intellectual feast!
Hour after hour, day after day,
Train after train runs every way,
Young recruits and old 'uns too,
In and out of Beverloo.
It would be a very fair shot
To suspect Louvain or Gerschot

23

(Or some intermediate station)
As their final destination.
Or will they dare, O *can* they mean
To venture onward to Malines
One asks oneself. I even feel
They may push on to Londerzeel
Along the road to far Courtrai
Where the flying fishes play –
(Youth, you know, will have its way)
Turning East my eyes are dazzled
By the spectacle of Hasselt:
Hanoverian and Saxon,
Some with picks and some with packs on.
Wurtemberger and Berliner,
Brunswickers from Bukovina,
Jagers, Uhlans, Ungedienste,
Landsturm crawling through Pepinster.
Dirty buggers from Belgrade
Pouring in by Welkenraedt.
Yet it really seems an age
Since a movement passed Liège!
How I miss the old effréné
Rough and tumble work at Chênée!
No one cares a row of pins
Any more for Guillemins,
And the latest German plans
Entirely boycott poor old Ans.
They have seen some awful tussles
Nowadays to get to Brussels;
Possibly they pass Namur,
(This is only conjecture)
Turn North West to Ottignies

And so to Schaerbeek – little geese!
As I feared there's not a sign
Of traffic on the southern line.
We pay an intellectual person
God knows what to spy at Hirson
And yet in spite of all his brain
He never spots a bloody train;
He merely gossips with the porters
And then reports a dozen mortars.
Vervins, Mézières, Sedan
Montmédy and Carignan
Might as well be in the sea
For all he does to earn his fee.
Well I think that ends my song;
If you find it overlong
You will pardon me, I trust,
I do but sing because I must.

Maurice Baring

August 1918 (in a French Village)

I hear the tinkling of a cattle bell,
In the broad stillness of the afternoon;
High in the cloudless haze the harvest moon
Is pallid as the phantom of a shell.

A girl is drawing water from a well,
I hear the clatter of her wooden shoon;
Two mothers to their sleeping babies croon,
And the hot village feels the drowsy spell.

Sleep, child, the Angel of Death his wings has
    spread;
His engines scour the land, the sea, the sky;
And all the weapons of Hell's armoury
Are ready for the blood that is their bread;
And many a thousand men to-night must die,
So many that they will not count the Dead.

R.H. Beckh

No Man's Land

Nine-thirty o'clock? Then over the top,
And mind to keep down when you see the flare
Of Very pistol searching the air.
Now, over you get; look out for the wire
In the borrow pit, and the empty tins,
They are meant for the Hun to bark his shins.
So keep well down and reserve your fire –
All over? Right: there's a gap just here
In the corkscrew wire, so just follow me;
If you keep well down there's nothing to fear.

     *   *   *

Then out we creep thro' the gathering gloom
Of no man's land, while the big guns boom
Right over our heads, and the rapid crack
Of the Lewis guns is answered back
By the German barking the same refrain
Of crack, crack, crack, all over again.

To the wistful eye from the parapet,
In the smiling sun of a summer's day,
'Twere a sin to believe that a bloody death
In those waving grasses lurking lay.
But now, 'neath the Very's fitful flares
'Keep still, my lads, and freeze like hares; –
All right, carry on, for we're out to enquire
If our friend the Hun's got a gap in his wire;
And he hasn't invited us out, you see,
So lift up your feet and follow me.'

* * *

Then, silent, we press with a noiseless tread
Thro' no man's land, but the sightless dead;
Aye, muffle your footsteps, well ye may,
For the mouldering corpses here decay
Whom no man owns but the King abhorred.
Grim Pluto, Stygia's over-lord.
Oh breathe a prayer for the sightless Dead
Who have bitten the dust 'neath the biting lead
Of the pitiless hail of the Maxim's fire,
'Neath the wash of shell in the well trod mire.
Ah well! But we've, too, got a job to be done,
For we've come to the wire of our friend, the Hun.
'Now, keep well down, lads; can you see any gap?

* * *

Not much, well the reference is wrong in the map'
So homeward we go thro' the friendly night.
That covers the no man's land from sight,
As muttering a noiseless prayer of praise,
We drop from the parapet into the bays.

28

William Eric Berridge

To a Rat

Caught on a piece of wire in a
communication trench 4.45 a.m. April 1916

Was it for this you came into the light?
Have you fulfilled Life's mission? You are free
For evermore from toil and misery,
Yet those who snared you, to their great delight,
Thought doubtless they were only doing right
In scheming to encompass your decease,
Forgetting they were bringing you to peace
And perfect joy and everlasting night.
Your course is ended here – I know not why
You seemed a loathsome, a pernicious creature;
You couldn't clothe us and we couldn't eat yer,
And so we mocked your humble destiny –
Yet life was merry, was it not, oh rat?
It must have been to one so sleek and fat.

Laurence Binyon

For the Fallen

With proud thanksgiving, a mother for her children,
England mourns for her dead across the sea.
Flesh of her flesh they were, spirit of her spirit,
Fallen in the cause of the free.

Solemn the drums thrill; Death august and royal
Sings sorrow up into immortal spheres.
There is music in the midst of desolation
And a glory that shines upon our tears.

They went with songs to the battle; they were young,
Straight of limb, true of eye, steady and aglow.
They were staunch to the end against odds
    uncounted;
They fell with their faces to the foe.

They shall grow not old, as we that are left grow old:
Age shall not weary them, nor the years condemn.
At the going down of the sun and in the morning
We will remember them.

They mingle not with their laughing comrades
    again;
They sit no more at familiar tables of home;
They have no lot in our labour of the day-time;
They sleep beyond England's foam.

But where our desires are and our hopes profound,
Felt as a well-spring that is hidden from sight,
To the innermost heart of their own land
      they are known
As the stars are known to the Night;

As the stars that shall be bright when we are dust,
Moving in marches upon the heavenly plain;
As the stars that are starry in the time of our
      darkness,
To the end, to the end, they remain.

John Peele Bishop

In the Dordogne

We stood up before day
and shaved by metal mirrors
in the faint flame of a faulty candle.

And we hurried down the wide stone stairs
with a clirr of spurr chains
on stone. And we thought
when the cocks crew
that the ghosts of a dead dawn
would rise and be off. But they stayed
under the window, crouched on the staircase,
the window now the colour of morning.

The colonel slept in the bed of Sully,
slept on: but we descended
and saw in a niche in the white wall
a Virgin and child, serene
who were stone: we saw sycamore:
three aged mages
scattering gifts of gold.
But when the wind blew, there were autumn odours
and the shadowed trees
had the dapplings of young fawns.

And each day one died or another
died: each week we sent out thousands
that returned by hundreds
wounded or gassed. And those that died
we buried close to the old wall
within a stone's throw of Perigord
under the tower of the troubadours.

And because we had courage;
because there was courage and youth
ready to be wasted; because we endured
and were prepared for all the endurance;
we thought something must come of it:
that the Virgin would raise her child and smile;
the trees gather up their gold and go;
that courage would avail something
and something we had never lost
be regained through wastage, by dying,
by burying the others under the English tower.

The colonel slept on in the bed of Sully
under the ravelling curtains: the leaves fell
and were blown away: the young men rotted
under the shadow of the tower
in a land of small clear silent streams
where the coming on of evening is
the letting down of blue and azure veils
over the clear and silent streams
delicately bordered by poplars.

Charles Walter Blackall

'Attack!'

You are standing watch in hand,
All waiting the command,
While your guns have got their trenches fairly set.
When they lengthen up the range,
You feel a trifle strange
As you clamber up the sand-bag parapet.

It's a case of do or die –
Still, you rather wonder why
Your mate drops down beside you with a screech;
But you're very soon aware,
When a bullet parts your hair,
That he's not the only pebble on the beach.

It's each man for himself,
For your Captain's on the shelf,
And you don't know if he's wounded or he's dead.
So never count the cost,
Of your comrades who are lost,
But keep the line on forging straight ahead.

The high-explosive shell
Has blown their wire to hell,
And their trench is like a muddy, bloody drain.
They are bolting left and right,
And the few that stay to fight –
Well, not many see their Fatherland again!

But there's one cove that you've missed,
And he cops you in the wrist
As you're stooping down to help a wounded chum.
Though you're feeling mighty faint,
As you're not a blooming saint,
You blow his blasted brains to kingdom come!

You've done your little job,
And you drop down with a sob,
For you're feeling half a man and half a wreck.
And you say a little prayer –
Which for you is rather rare –
For you got it in the arm, and not the neck.

When the evening shadows fall,
You do your best to crawl,
Till the stretcher-bearers find you in a creek.
Then you feel as right as rain,
And forget the aching pain,
For you'll see Old England's shores within a week.

Edmund Blunden

The Zonnebeke Road

Morning, if this late withered light can claim
Some kindred with that merry flame
Which the young day was wont to fling through
    space!
Agony stares from each grey face.
And yet the day is come; stand down! stand down!
Your hands unclasp from rifles while you can;
The frost has pierced them to the bended bone?
Why see old Stevens there, that iron man,
Melting the ice to shave his grotesque chin!
Go ask him, shall we win?
I never likes this bay, some foolish fear
Caught me the first time that I came here;
That dugout fallen in awakes, perhaps
Some formless haunting of some corpse's chaps.
True, and wherever we have held the line,
There were such corners, seeming-saturnine
For no good cause.

Now where the Haymarket starts,
There is no place for soldiers with weak hearts;
The minenwerfers have it to the inch.
Look, how the snow-dust whisks along the road
Piteous and silly; the stones themselves must flinch
In this east wind; the low sky like a load
Hangs over, a dead-weight. But what a pain
Must gnaw where its clay cheek
Crushes the shell-chopped trees that fang the plain –
The ice-bound throat gulps out a gargoyle shriek.
That wretched wire before the village line
Rattles like rusty brambles on dead bine,
And there the daylight oozes into dun;
Black pillars, those are trees where roadways run
Even Ypres now would warm our souls; fond fool,
Our tour's but one night old, seven more to cool!
O screaming dumbness, o dull clashing death,
Shreds of dead grass and willows, homes and men,
Watch as you will, men clench their chattering teeth
And freeze you back with that one hope, disdain.

Edmund Blunden

1916 seen from 1921

Tired with dull grief, grown old before my day,
I sit in solitude and only hear
Long silent laughters, murmurings of dismay,
The lost intensities of hope and fear;
In those old marshes yet the rifles lie,
On the thin breastwork flutter the grey rags,
The very books I read are there – and I
Dead as the men I loved, wait while life drags

Its wounded length from those sad streets of war
Into green places here, that were my own;
But now what once was mine is mine no more,
I seek such neighbours here and I find none.
With such strong gentleness and tireless will
Those ruined houses seared themselves in me,
Passionate I look for their dumb story still,
And the charred stub outspeaks the living tree.

I rise up at the singing of a bird
And scarcely knowing slink along the lane,
I dare not give a soul a look or word
Where all have homes and none's at home in vain:
Deep red the rose burned in the grim redoubt,
The self-sown wheat around was like a flood,
In the hot path the lizard lolled time out,
The saints in broken shrines were bright as blood.

Sweet Mary's shrine between the sycamores!
There we would go, my friend of friends and I,
And snatch long moments from the grudging wars,
Whose dark made light intense to see them by.
Shrewd bit the morning fog, the whining shots
Spun from the wrangling wire: then in warm swoon
The sun hushed all but the cool orchard plots,
We crept in the tall grass and slept till noon.

Rupert Brooke

Peace

Now, God be thanked Who has matched us with
    His hour,
And caught our youth, and wakened us from
    sleeping,
With hand made sure, clear eye, and sharpened
    power,
To turn, as swimmers into cleanness leaping,
Glad from a world grown old and cold and weary,
Leave the sick hearts that honour could not move,
And half-men, and their dirty songs and dreary,
And all the little emptiness of love!

Oh! we who have known shame, we have found
    release there,
Where there's no ill, no grief, but sleep has mending,
Nought broken save this body, lost but breath;
Nothing to shake the laughing heart's long peace
    there
But only agony, and that has ending;
And the worst friend and enemy is but Death.

Rupert Brooke

The Dead

Blow out, you bugles, over the rich Dead!
  There's none of these so lonely and poor of old,
  But, dying, has made us rarer gifts than gold.
These laid the world away; poured out the red
Sweet wine of youth; gave up the years to be
  Of work and joy, and that unhoped serene,
  That men call age; and those who would have
    been,
Their sons, they gave, their immortality.

Blow, bugles, blow! They brought us, for our dearth,
  Holiness, lacked so long, and Love, and Pain.
Honour has come back, as a king, to earth,
  And paid his subjects with a royal wage;
And Nobleness walks in our ways again;
  And we have come into our heritage.

Rupert Brooke

The Soldier

If I should die, think only this of me:
That there's some corner of a foreign field
That is for ever England. There shall be
In that rich earth a richer dust concealed;
A dust whom England bore, shaped, made aware,
Gave, once, her flowers to love, her ways to roam,
A body of England's, breathing English air,
Washed by the rivers, blest by suns of home.

And think, this heart, all evil shed away,
A pulse in the eternal mind, no less
Gives somewhere back the thoughts by England
    given;
Her sights and sounds; dreams happy as her day;
And laughter, learnt of friends; and gentleness,
In hearts at peace, under an English heaven.

Edward Carpenter

Lieutenant Tattoon, M.C.

The case of Lieutenant Tattoon, M.C.
  Is worthy of some remark.
He thought (and one should not think, you see)
That the War which was to make people free
  Was now being fought in the dark.

For at first (he said) our aims were clear,
  Men gave their lives with gladness
To save small nations from the fear
Of Tyrants who would domineer
  And doom mankind to madness.

Our rulers had claimed – and rightly I ween –
  That the Germans must be 'broken';
But afterwards, What that word might mean,
And what sort of peace was to supervene,
  Were things which they left unspoken.

And no one knew whatever on Earth
  Our present objective and aim were,
And whether the loss and deadly dearth
Of another Million of lives was worth
  Some gains in Mesopotamia.

These were the thoughts of Lieutenant Tattoon. –
  Of course it was very improper,
But he actually gave them expression, and soon
Found out he was trying to jump the Moon
  And only coming a cropper!

For to say what you mean is all right as a rule
   In a far oversea Dominion,
But at home or under the Prussian school
It is not safe – and a man is a fool
   Even to have an opinion.

A Medical Board sat on him, in state
   (No wonder they looked so solemn);
His sins were entered upon the slate
With every lapse detailed to date –
   And they added up the Column.

He thought – which for a Lieutenant was rash;
   He spoke, but should have kept silence;
He treated Imperial talk as trash,
And considered the honour before the cash
   Which might come to the British Islands.

'Twas insubordination, they said,
   And he surely must be crazy –
Yet there he stood, in mien well-bred;
Collected and calm, with clean-cut head,
   And looking as fit as a daisy.

An M.C. too – so what could they do?
   'Twas a most provoking and strange craze.
Yet to put him in prison a storm would brew
Of wrath – the mere proposal to mew
   A hero in Woking or Strangeways!

For half an hour (as once in Heaven)
  Silence fell on the folk assembled;
Till by one inspired the stillness was riven:
' 'Twas nervous shock.' The cue was given –
  And the whole Court gaily dissembled.

'Poor fellow!' they said, ' 'Twas nervous strain,
  He's a subject for our pity;
Let him to Hospital go, till his brain
Is healed, and there's no danger again
  That he will repeat that ditty.'

To a Shell-shock ward then he was sent,
  And there he was kindly treated
And even indulged to the top of his bent; –
But there ever since he has safely been pent,
  And his words have not been repeated.

G.K. Chesterton

Elegy in a Country Churchyard

The men that worked for England
They have their graves at home:
And bees and birds of England
About the cross can roam.

But they that fought for England,
Following a falling star,
Alas, alas for England
They have their graves afar.

And they that rule in England,
In stately conclave met,
Alas, alas for England
They have no graves as yet.

Margaret Postgate Cole

The Veteran

We came upon him sitting in the sun,
    Blinded by war, and left. And past the fence
There came young soldiers from the Hand and
        Flower,
    Asking advice of his experience.

And he said this, and that, and told them tales,
    And all the nightmares of each empty head
Blew into air; then, hearing us beside,
    'Poor chaps, how'd they know what it's like?'
        he said.

And we stood there, and watched him as he sat,
    Turning his sockets where they went away,
Until it came to one of us to ask
    'And you're – how old?'
        'Nineteen, the third of May.'

Leslie Coulson

The Rainbow

I watch the white dawn gleam,
To the thunder of hidden guns.
  I hear the hot shells scream
Through skies as sweet as a dream
Where the silver dawnbreak runs.
    And stabbing of light
  Scorches the virginal white.
But I feel in my being the old, high, sanctified thrill,
  And I thank the gods that dawn is beautiful still.

From death that hurtles by
  I crouch in the trench day-long
But up to a cloudless sky
From the ground where our dead men lie
  A brown lark soars in song.
    Through the tortured air,
  Rent by the shrapnel's flare,
Over the troubless dead he carols his fill,
And I thank the gods that the birds are beautiful still.

Where the parapet is low
  And level with the eye
Poppies and cornflowers glow
And the corn sways to and fro
  In a pattern against the sky.
    The gold stalks hide
  Bodies of men who died
Charging at dawn through the dew to be killed or
    to kill.
  I thank the gods that the flowers are beautiful still.

When night falls dark we creep
  In silence to our dead.
  We dig a few feet deep
And leave them there to sleep –
  But blood at night is red,
  Yea, even at night,
And a dead man's face is white.
And I dry my hands, that are also trained to kill,
And I look at the stars – for the stars are beautiful
    still.

Leslie Coulson

War

Where war has left its wake of whitened bone,
Soft stems of summer grass shall wave again,
And all the blood that war has ever strewn
        Is but a passing stain.

Leslie Coulson

Who Made the Law?

Who made the Law that men should die in
    meadows?
Who spake the word that blood should splash in
    lanes?
Who gave it forth that gardens should be bone-
    yards?
Who spread the hills with flesh, and blood, and
    brains?
Who made the Law?

Who made the Law that Death should stalk the
    village?
Who spake the word to kill among the sheaves?
Who gave it forth that death should lurk in
    hedgerows?
Who flung the dead among the fallen leaves?
Who made the Law?

Those who return shall find that peace endures,
Find old things old, and know the things they knew,
Walk in the garden, slumber by the fireside,
Share the peace of dawn, and dream amid the dew –
Those who return.

Those who return shall till the ancient pastures,
Clean-hearted men shall guide the plough-horse
    reins,
Some shall grow apples and flowers in the valleys,
Some shall go courting in summer down the lanes –
Those Who Return.

But who made the Law? the Trees shall whisper to
    him:
'See, see the blood – the splashes on our bark!'
Walking the meadows, he shall hear bones crackle,
And fleshless mouths shall gibber in silent lanes at
    dark.
Who made the Law?

Who made the Law? At noon upon the hillside
His ears shall hear a moan, his cheeks shall feel a
    breath,
And all along the valleys, past gardens, croft, and
    homesteads,
He who made the Law,
  He who made the Law,
He who made the Law shall walk along with Death.
  Who made the Law?

Jeffery Day

On the Wings of the Morning

A sudden roar, a mighty rushing sound,
  a jolt or two, a smoothly sliding rise,
a tumbled blur of disappearing ground,
    and then all sense of motion slowly dies.
      Quiet and calm, the earth slips past below,
      as underneath a bridge still waters flow.

My turning wing inclines towards the ground;
  The ground itself glides up with graceful swing
and at the plane's far tip twirls slowly round,
    then drops from sight again beneath the wing
      to slip away serenely as before,
      a cubist-patterned carpet on the floor.

Hills gently sink and valleys gently fill.
  The flattened fields grow ludicrously small;
slowly they pass beneath and slower still
    until they hardly seem to move at all.
      Then suddenly they disappear from sight,
      hidden by fleeting wisps of faded white.

The wing-tips, faint and dripping, dimly show,
  blurred by the wreaths of mist that intervene.
Weird, half-seen shadows flicker to and fro
    across the pallid fog-bank's blinding screen.
      At last the choking mists release their hold,
      and all the world is silver, blue, and gold.

The air is clear, more clear than sparkling wine;
   compared with this, wine is a turgid brew.
The far horizon makes a clean-cut line
   between the silver and the depthless blue.
      Out of the snow-white level reared on high
      glittering hills surge up to meet the sky.

Outside the wind screen's shelter gales may race:
   but in the seat a cool and gentle breeze
blows steadily upon my grateful face.
   As I sit motionless and at my ease,
      contented just to loiter in the sun
      and gaze around me till the day is done.

And so I sit, half sleeping, half awake,
   dreaming a happy dream of golden days,
until at last, with a reluctant shake
   I rouse myself, and with a lingering gaze
      at all the splendour of the shining plain
      make ready to come down to earth again.

The engine stops: a pleasant silence reigns –
   silence, not broken, but intensified
by the soft, sleepy wires' insistent strains,
   that rise and fall, as with a sweeping glide
      I slither down the well-oiled sides of space,
      towards a lower, less enchanted place.

The clouds draw nearer, changing as they come.
  Now, like a flash, fog grips me by the throat.
Down goes the nose: at once the wires' low hum
  begins to rise in volume and in note,
    till, as I hurtle from the choking cloud
    it swells into a scream, high-pitched, and loud.

The scattered hues and shades of green and brown
  fashion themselves into the land I know,
turning and twisting, as I spiral down
  towards the landing-ground; till, skimming low,
    I glide with slackening speed across the ground,
    and come to rest with lightly grating sound.

Alec de Candole

And if a Bullet

And if a bullet in the midst of strife
Should still the pulse of this unquiet life,
'Twere well: be death an everlasting rest,
I oft could yearn for it, by cares opprest;
And be't a night that brings another day,
I still could go rejoicing on my way,
Desiring in no phantom heav'n to dwell,
Nor scared with terror of any phantom hell,
But gazing now I find not death a curse
Better than life perchance, at least not worse;
Only the fierce and rending agony,
The torment of the flesh about to die,
Affrights my soul; but that shall pass anon,
And death's repose or strife be found, that gone;
Only with that last earthly ill to cope
God grant me strength, and I go forth with hope.

Oliphant Down

Picardy Parodies No. 2 (W.B. Y—ts)

I will arise and go now, and go to Picardy,
And a new trench-line hold there, of clay and shell-
    holes made,
No dug-outs shall I have there, nor a hive for the
    Lewis G.,
But live on top in the b. loud glade.

And I may cease to be there, for peace comes
    dropping slow.
Dropping from the mouth of the Minnie to where
    the sentry sings;
There noon is high explosive, and night a gunfire
    glow,
And evening full of torpedoes' wings.

I will arise and go now, though always night and day
I'll feel dark waters lapping with low sounds by the
    store,
Where all our bombs grow rusty and countless
    S.A.A.;
I'll feel it in my trench-feet sore.

F.S. Flint

Lament

The young men of the world
Are condemned to death.
They have been called up to die
For the crime of their fathers.

The young men of the world,
The growing, the ripening fruit,
Have been torn from their branches,
While the memory of the blossom
Is sweet in women's hearts;
They have been cast for a cruel purpose
Into the mashing-press and furnace.

The young men of the world
Look into each other's eyes,
And read there the same words:
Not yet! Not yet!
But soon perhaps, and perhaps certain.

Clifford Flower

A Calm Night at the Front

The rough Profanity is lost in sleep,
   The body rests, the mind is dreaming:
The men on guard their watch do keep,
   The moon's rays gently beaming.

The rifle fire has died away,
   All silent now; the moon on high
Would set a truce until the day,
   God staying the hand of destiny.

I think that when those dark'ning clouds
   Have gathered up the tempest's lust,
The blackness of the night in shrouds
   Will show how mean the human trust.

The fiend of war that hides in wait
   Will venture forth in boom of guns
And rattling lead, a 'Hymn of Hate',
   Wild dirge of men – just women's sons.

I do not doubt there is an end
  To all this slaughter of the brave
By monster forms, who tear and rend
  The innocent before the grave.

O, womenfolk of British lands,
  Who toil and sweat in holiest cause,
O, raise in prayer your clasped hands
  That men may see the curse of wars.

A single star-light held in space
  Has filled the trench with radiance white,
A cautious soldier hides his face,
  Somebody's calling, so, 'Good Night'.

Gilbert Frankau

The Deserter

'I'm sorry I done it, Major.'
We bandaged the livid face;
And led him out, ere the wan sun rose,
To die his death of disgrace.

The bolt-heads locked to the cartridge;
The rifles steadied to rest,
As cold stock nestled at colder cheek
And foresight lined on the breast.

'Fire!' called the Sergeant-Major.
The muzzles flamed as he spoke:
And the shameless soul of a nameless man
Went up in the cordite-smoke.

H. Rex Freston

October 31st, 1915

It is the last morning of October!
And the wind hisses among the ragged leaves;
The trees look shabby and cold.
The window-pane is splashed all over with
    raindrops;
And raindrops run down like tears on the ivy's face,
Pause a moment, and fall.

Where is everybody? What are they doing?
Are they walking about in the rain?
The sound of the church bells is blown about on the
    wind,
Now loud; now low;
Very far; suddenly, strangely near; and very far again:
A lot of people must be going to church –
I don't like the way people look at you as you go in,
It makes me feel so uncomfortable.

Out in France, a lot of men are standing in the
    trenches,
Most of them are wearing old caps.
And their unshaved faces are half hidden in dirty
    mufflers.
They all look very ugly, and are cursing the rain –
In a week or two I shall be out there with them –
What will happen if I never come back again?

It is most annoying that I shall not have time to
    express myself,
Owing to this war,
I shall not have time to make people angry with me
    for telling the truth,
O those respectable people! Those well-to-do, smug,
    self-satisfied men and women!
How daintily, finely they dress! Their voices are most
    refined.
But it would be splendid to take all their money
    away,
And make them live on eighteen shillings a week,
And work for it!

After I am dead,
And have become part of the soil of France,
This much remember of me:
I was a great sinner, a great lover, and life puzzled me
    very much.
Ah love! I would have died for love!
Love can do so much, both rightly and wrongly.
It remembers mothers, and little children,
And lots of other things.
O men unborn, I go now, my work unfinished!
I pass on the problem to you: the world will hate
    you: be brave!

H. Rex Freston

To A.M.

(Killed in Flanders)

Now you are dead, I dare not read
   That letter that you sent to me
Before you went: my heart would bleed
   If I that writing now should see.

For I should dream how, long ago,
   We walked those careless Oxford ways,
When Cherwell's banks were all aglow
   With hawthorn and with reddening mays.

And see, as once I used to see,
   St Mary's spire against the sky:
And hear you laugh and call to me
   As I came slowly up the High.

Crosbie Garstin

Chemin des Dames

In silks and satins the ladies went
Where the breezes sighed and the poplars bent,
Taking the air of a Sunday morn
Midst the red of poppies and gold of corn –
Flowery ladies in stiff brocades,
With negro pages and serving-maids,
In scarlet coach or in gilt sedan,
With brooch and buckle and flounce and fan,
Patch and powder and trailing scent,
Under the trees the ladies went –
Lovely ladies that gleamed and glowed,
As they took the air on the Ladies' Road.

Boom of thunder and lightning flash –
The torn earth rocks to the barrage crash;
The bullets whine and the bullets sing
From the mad machine-guns chattering;
Black smoke rolling across the mud,
Trenches plastered with flesh and blood –
The blue ranks lock with the ranks of grey,
Stab and stagger and sob and sway;
The living cringe from the shrapnel bursts,
The dying moan of their burning thirsts,
Moan and die in the gulping slough –
Where are the butterfly ladies now?

Wilfrid Gibson

Back

They ask me where I've been,
And what I've done and seen.
But what can I reply
Who know it wasn't I,
But someone just like me,
Who went across the sea
And with my head and hands
Killed men in foreign lands …
Though I must bear the blame,
Because he bore my name.

Robert Graves

A Dead Boche

To you who'd read my songs of War
And only hear of blood and fame,
I'll say (you've heard it said before)
   'War's Hell!' and if you doubt the same,
To-day I found in Mametz Wood
A certain cure for lust of blood:

Where, propped against a shattered trunk,
   In a great mess of things unclean,
Sat a dead Boche; he scowled and stunk
   With clothes and face a sodden green,
Big-bellied, spectacled, crop-haired,
Dribbling black blood from nose and beard.

Robert Graves

The Last Post

The bugler sent a call of high romance –
'Lights out! Lights out!' to the deserted square.
On the thin brazen notes he threw a prayer,
'God, if it's *this* for me next time in France …
O spare the phantom bugle as I lie
Dead in the gas and smoke and roar of guns,
Dead in a row with the other broken ones
Lying so stiff and still under the sky,
Jolly young Fusiliers too good to die.'

Julian Grenfell

Into Battle

The naked earth is warm with spring,
    And with green grass and bursting trees
Leans to the sun's gaze glorying,
    And quivers in the sunny breeze;
And life is colour and warmth and light,
    And a striving evermore for these;
And he is dead who will not fight;
    And who dies fighting has increase.

The fighting man shall from the sun
    Take warmth, and life from the glowing earth;
Speed with the light-foot winds to run,
    And with the trees to newer birth;
And find, when fighting shall be done,
    Great rest, and fullness after dearth.

All the bright company of Heaven
    Hold him in their high comradeship,
The Dog-Star, and the Sisters Seven,
    Orion's Belt and sworded hip.

The woodland trees that stand together,
    They stand to him each one a friend;
They gently speak in the windy weather;
    They guide to valley and ridge's end.

The kestrel hovering by day,
    And the little owls that call by night,
Bid him be swift and keen as they,
    As keen of ear, as swift of sight.

The blackbird sings to him, 'Brother, brother,
   If this be the last song you shall sing,
Sing well, for you may not sing another;
   Brother, sing.'

In dreary, doubtful, waiting hours,
   Before the brazen frenzy starts,
The horses show him nobler powers;
   O patient eyes, courageous hearts!

And when the burning moment breaks,
   And all things else are out of mind,
And only joy of battle takes
   Him by the throat, and makes him blind,

Through joy and blindness he shall know,
   Not caring much to know, that still
Nor lead nor steel shall reach him, so
   That it be not the Destined Will.

The thundering line of battle stands,
   And in the air death moans and sings;
But Day shall clasp him with strong hands,
   And Night shall fold him in soft wings.

Julian Grenfell

A Prayer for Those on the Staff

Fighting in mud, we turn to Thee,
In these dread times of battle, Lord.
To keep us safe, if so may be,
From shrapnel, snipers, shell, and sword.

But not on us, for we are men
Of meaner clay, who fight in clay,
but on the Staff, the Upper Ten,
Depends the issue of the Day.

The staff is working with its brains,
While we are sitting in the trench;
The Staff the universe ordains
(subject to Thee and General French).

God help the staff – especially
The young ones, many of them sprung
From our high aristocracy;
Their task is hard, and they are young.

O Lord, who mad'st all things to be,
And madest some things very good,
Please keep the extra A.D.C.
From horrid scenes, and sight of blood.

See that his eggs are newly laid,
Not tinged as some of them – with green;
And let no nasty draughts invade
The windows of his Limousine.

When he forgets to buy the bread,
When there are no more minerals,
Preserve his smooth well-oiled head
From wrath of caustic Generals.

O Lord, who mad'st all things to be,
And hatest nothing thou has made,
Please keep the extra A.D.C.
Out of the sun and in the shade.

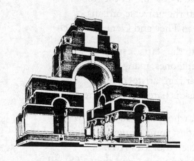

Ivor Gurney

De Profundis

If only this fear would leave me I could dream of
    Crickley Hill
And a hundred thousand thoughts of home would
    visit my heart in sleep;
But here the peace is shattered all day by the devil's
    will,
    And the guns bark night-long to spoil the velvet
    silence deep.

O who could think that once we drank in quiet inns
    and cool
    And saw brown oxen trooping the dry sands to
    slake
Their thirst at the river flowing, or plunged in a
    silver pool
    To shake the sleepy drowse off before well awake?

We are stale here, we are covered body and soul and
    mind
    With mire of the trenches, close clinging and foul.
We have left our old inheritance, our Paradise
    behind,
    And clarity is lost to us and cleanness of soul.

O blow here, you dusk-airs and breaths of half-light,
   And comfort despairs of your darlings that long
Night and day for sound of your bells, or a sight
   Of your tree-bordered lanes, land of blossom and
      song.

Autumn will be here soon, but the road of coloured
      leaves
   Is not for us, the up and down highway where go
Earth's pilgrims to wonder where Malvern upheaves
   That blue-emerald splendour under great clouds
      of snow.

Some day we'll fill in trenches, level the land and
      turn
   Once more joyful faces to the country where trees
Bear thickly for good drink, where strong sunsets
      burn
   Huge bonfires of glory – O God, send us peace!

Hard it is for men of moors or fens to endure
   Exile and hardship, or the northland grey-drear;
But we of the rich plain of sweet airs and pure,
   Oh! Death would take so much from us, how
      should we not fear?

Ivor Gurney

Portrait of a Coward

True he'd have fought to death if the Germans
    came –
But an hours battering after a days battering
Brought his soul down to quivering, with small
    shame.
And he was fit to run, if his chance had come.
But Gloucesters of more sterner frame and spirit
Kept him in place without reproach, (sweet blood
    inherit
From hills and nature) said no word and kept him
    there.
True, he'd have fought to death, but Laventie's
    needing
Was a nerve to hide the pain of the soul bleeding –
Say nothing, and nothing ever of God to beg.
He hurt more, did fatigues, and was friend to share
What food was not his need; of enemies not
    heeding.
Everybody was glad – (but determined to hide the
    bad)
When he took courage at wiremending and shot his
    leg,
And got to Blighty, no man saying word of denying.

Ivor Gurney

Strange Hells

There are strange Hells within the minds War made
Not so often, not so humiliatingly afraid
As one would have expected – the racket and fear
    guns made.

One Hell the Gloucester soldiers they quite put out;
Their first bombardment, when in combined black
    shout
Of fury, guns aligned, they ducked lower their heads
And sang with diaphragms fixed beyond all dreads,
That tin and stretched-wire tinkle, that blither of
    tune;
'Après la guerre fini' till Hell all had come down,
Twelve-inch, six-inch, and eighteen-pounders
    hammering Hell's thunders.

Where are they now on State-doles, or showing
    shop-patterns
Or walking town to town sore in borrowed tatterns
Or begged. Some civic routine one never learns.
The heart burns – but has to keep out of face how
    heart burns.

Ivor Gurney

The Silent One

Who died on the wires, and hung there, one of two –
Who for his hours of life had chattered through
Infinite lovely chatter of Bucks accent:
Yet faced unbroken wires; stepped over, and went
A noble fool, faithful to his stripes – and ended.
But I weak, hungry, and willing only for the chance
Of line – to fight in the line, lay down under
    unbroken
Wires, and saw the flashes and kept unshaken,
Till the politest voice – a finicking accent, said:
'Do you think you might crawl through there: there's
    a hole'
Darkness, shot at: I smiled, as politely replied –
'I'm afraid not, Sir.' There was no hole no way to be
    seen
Nothing but chance of death, after tearing of clothes.
Kept flat, and watched the darkness, hearing bullets
    whizzing –
And thought of music – and swore deep heart's deep
    oaths
(Polite to God) and retreated and came on again,
Again retreated – and a second time faced the screen.

Ivor Gurney

The Target

I shot him, and it had to be
One of us! 'Twas him or me.
'Couldn't be helped' and none can blame
Me, for you would do the same.

My mother, she can't sleep for fear
Of what might be a-happening here
To me. Perhaps it might be best
To die, and set her fears at rest.

For worst is worst, and worry's done.
Perhaps he was the only son …
Yet God keeps still, and does not say
A word of guidance anyway.

Well, if they get me, first I'll find
That boy, and tell him all my mind,
And see who felt the bullet worst,
And ask his pardon, if I durst.

All's a tangle. Here's my job.
A man might rave, or shout, or sob;
And God He takes no sort of heed.
This is a bloody mess indeed.

Ivor Gurney

To His Love

He's gone, and all our plans
   Are useless indeed.
We'll walk no more on Cotswold
   Where the sheep feed
   Quietly and take no heed.

His body that was so quick
   Is not as you
Knew it, on Severn river
   Under the blue
   Driving our small boat through.

You would not know him now …
   But still he died
Nobly, so cover him over
   With violets of pride
   Purple from Severn side.

Cover him, cover him soon!
   And with thick-set
Masses of memoried flowers –
   Hide that red wet
   Thing I must somehow forget.

Ivor Gurney

To the Prussians of England

When I remember plain heroic strength
And shining virtue shown by Ypres pools,
Then read the blither written by knaves for fools
In praise of English soldiers lying at length,
Who purely dream what England shall be made
Gloriously new, free of the old stains
By us, who pay the price that must be paid,
Will freeze all winter over Ypres plains.
Our silly dreams of peace you put aside
And brotherhood of man, for you will see
An armed mistress, braggart of the tide,
Her children slaves, under your mastery.
We'll have a word there too, and forge a knife,
Will cut the cancer threatens England's life.

Thomas Hardy

Channel Firing

That night your great guns, unawares,
Shook all our coffins as we lay,
And broke the chancel window-squares,
We thought it was the Judgment-day.

And sat upright. While drearisome
Arose the howl of wakened hounds:
The mouse let fall the altar-crumb,
The worms drew back into the mounds,

The glebe cow drooled. Till God called, 'No;
It's gunnery practice out at sea
Just as before you went below;
The world is as it used to be:

'All nations striving strong to make
Red war yet redder. Mad as hatters
They do no more for Christés sake
Than you who are helpless in such matters.

'That this is not the judgment-hour
For some of them's a blessed thing,
For if it were they'd have to scour
Hell's floor for so much threatening …

'Ha, ha. It will be warmer when
I blow the trumpet (if indeed
I ever do; for you are men,
And rest eternal sorely need).'

So down we lay again. 'I wonder,
Will the world ever saner be,'
Said one, 'than when He sent us under
In our indifferent century!'

And many a skeleton shook his head.
'Instead of preaching forty year,'
My neighbour Parson Thirdly said,
'I wish I had stuck to pipes and beer.'

Again the guns disturbed the hour,
Roaring their readiness to avenge,
As far inland as Stourton Tower,
And Camelot, and starlit Stonehenge.

Thomas Hardy

Men Who March Away

Song of the Soldiers

What of the faith and fire within us
Men who march away
Ere the barn-cocks say
Night is growing grey,
To hazards whence no tears can win us;
What of the faith and fire within us
Men who march away!

Is it a purblind prank, O think you,
Friend with the musing eye
Who watch us stepping by,
With doubt and dolorous sigh?
Can much pondering so hoodwink you?
Is it a purblind prank, O think you,
Friend with the musing eye?

Nay. We see well what we are doing,
Though some may not see –
Dalliers as they be –
England's need are we;
Her distress would leave us rueing:
Nay. We well see what we are doing,
Though some may not see!

In our heart of hearts believing
Victory crowns the just,
And that braggarts must
Surely bite the dust,
Press we to the field ungrieving,
In our heart of hearts believing
Victory crowns the just.

Hence the faith and fire within us
Men who march away
Ere the barn-cocks say
Night is growing grey,
To hazards whence no tears can win us;
Hence the faith and fire within us
Men who march away.

John Hay Maitland Hardyman

From a Base Hospital in France

Christ! I am blind! God give me strength to bear
That which I most have dreaded all my days:
The palsied shuffling, grasping air,
The moving prison five foot square,
The haunting step that isn't there –
These pictures dance before my sightless gaze …

A.P. Herbert

Beaucourt Revisited

I wandered down to Beaucourt; I took the river
    track,
And saw the lines we lived in before the Bosche
    went back;
But peace was now in pottage, the front was far
    ahead,
The front had journeyed Eastward and only left the
    dead.

And I thought how long we'd lain there and watched
    across the wire
While the guns roared round the valley and set the
    sky on fire.
But now there are houses in Hamel and tents in the
    Vale of Hell,
And a camp at Suicide Corner where half a regiment
    fell.

The new troops follow after and tread the land we
    won,
To them it's so much hillside we wrested from the
    Hun.
We only walk with reverence this solemn mile of
    mud;
The shell holes hold our history and half of them
    our blood.

Here at the head of Pace Street was death to show
  your face;
To me it seemed like magic to linger in the place;
For me how many spirits hung round the Kentish
  Caves
But the new men see no spirits, they only see the
  graves.

I found the half dug ditches we fashioned for the
  fight,
We left a score of men there, young James was killed
  that night;
I saw the starshells staring, I heard the bullets hail,
But the new troops pass unheeding, they never heard
  the tale.

I crossed the blood red ribbon that once was no-
  mans-land,
I saw a misty daybreak and a creeping minute hand;
And here the lads went over, and here was
  Harmsworth shot,
And here was William lying, but the new men know
  them not.

And I said, 'There is the river and still the stiff stark
  trees.
To treasure hear our story, but there are only these.'
But under the white wood crosses the dead men
  answered low,
'The new men know not Beaucourt, but we are here,
  we know.'

John Hobson

The Machine Gun

Here do I lie,
    Couched in the grass
With my machine-gun
Loaded, lurking, ready.
Fast must he fly
    Who fain would pass.
Sure is my eye,
My hand is steady.

The sky is blue,
    The planes are humming,
But my machine gun
Waits and watches ever.
Fair is the view,
Though guns be drumming,
    Though yonder hill from this
King Death doth sever.

All around me
    Blows the dogrose;
But my machine gun
Hidden is in daisies,
    Lurking is he
    Where the grass grows,
Peering ever forth
Through summer hazes.

Come ye who may,
    Foeman in air, or earth!
For my machine gun
Sings for you alone,
And in his lay
    To silvery death gives birth.
Now lifts now lowers he
His deadly tone.

Speak him not fair!
    He peers, but does not see
My black machine gun
Who waits from night to morn.
Silent in his low lair,
    Mighty, unseen and free,
Dealer of death and wounds
To those who scorn.

Here do I lie,
    Hidden by grass and flowers,
With my machine gun,
Ghost of modern war.
The sun floats high,
    The moon through deep blue hours,
I watch with my machine gun
At Death's grim door.

William Hodgson

Back to Rest

(Composed while marching to Rest Camp
after severe fighting at Loos)

A leaping wind from England,
The skies without a stain,
Clean cut against the morning
Slim poplars after rain,
The foolish noise of sparrows
And starlings in the wood –
After the grime of battle
We know that these are good.

Death whining down from Heaven,
Death roaring from the ground,
Death stinking in the nostril,
Death shrill in every sound,
Doubting we charged and conquered –
Hopeless we struck and stood.
Now when the fight is ended
We know that it was good.

We that have seen the strongest
Cry like a beaten child,
The sanest eyes unholy,
The cleanest hands defiled,
We that have known the heart blood
Less than the lees of wine,
We that have seen men broken,
We know man is divine.

William Hodgson

Before Action

By all the glories of the day
   And the cool evening's benison,
By that last sunset touch that lay
   Upon the hills when day was done,
By beauty lavishly outpoured
   And blessings carelessly received,
By all the days that I have lived
   Make me a soldier, Lord.

By all of man's hopes and fears,
   And all the wonders poets sing,
The laughter of unclouded years,
   And every sad and lovely thing;
By the romantic ages stored
   With high endeavour that was his,
By all his mad catastrophes
   Make me a man, O Lord.

I, that on my familiar hill
   Saw with uncomprehending eyes
A hundred of Thy sunsets spill
   Their fresh and sanguine sacrifice,
Ere the sun swings his noonday sword
   Must say goodbye to all of this; –
By all delights that I shall miss,
   Help me to die, O Lord.

William Hodgson

England to Her Sons

Sons of mine, I hear you thrilling
To the trumpet call of war;
Gird ye then, I give you freely
As I gave your sires before,
All the noblest of the children I in love and anguish
    bore.

Free in service, wise in justice,
Fearing but dishonour's breath;
Steeled to suffer uncomplaining
Loss and failure, pain and death;
Strong in faith that sees the issue and in hope that
    triumpheth.

Go, and may the God of battles
You in His good guidance keep:
And if He in wisdom giveth
Unto His beloved sleep,
I accept it nothing asking, save a little space to weep.

William Hodgson

Reverie

At home they see on Skiddaw
His royal purple lie
And Autumn up in Newlands
Arrayed in russet die,
Or under burning woodland
The still lake's gramarye.
And far off and grim and sable
The menace of the Gable,
Lifts up his stark aloofness
Against the western sky.

At vesper-time in Durham
The level evening falls
Upon the shadowy river
That slides by ancient walls,
Where out of crannied turrets
The mellow belfry calls.
And there sleep brings forgetting
And morning no regretting,
And love is laughter-wedded
To health in happy halls.

But here are blood and blisters
And thirst as hard as sand
An interminable travelling
Interminable land;
And stench and filth and sickness
And hate by hardship fanned.
The haunt of desolation
Wherein a desperate nation
Writhes in the grip of murder's
Inexorable hand.

Above the graves of heroes
The wooden crosses grow,
That shall no more see Durham
Nor any place they know,
Where fell tops face the morning
And great winds blow;
Who loving as none other
The land that is their mother
Unfaltering renounced her
Because they loved her so.

A.E. Housman

Here Dead We Lie

Here dead we lie because we did not choose
To live and shame the land from which we sprung.

Life, to be sure, is nothing much to lose;
But young men think it is, and we were young.

T.E. Hulme

Trenches: St Eloi

Over the flat slope of St Eloi
A wide wall of sandbags.
Night,
In the silence desultory men
Pottering over small fires, cleaning their mess-tins.
To and fro, from the lines,
Men walk as on Piccadilly,
Making paths in the dark,
Through scattered dead horses,
Over a dead Belgian's belly.

Philip Johnstone

High Wood

Ladies and gentlemen, this is High Wood,
Called by the French, Bois des Fourneaux,
The famous spot which in Nineteen-Sixteen,
July, August and September was the scene
Of long and bitterly contested strife,
By reason of its High commanding site.
Observe the effect of shell-fire in the trees
Standing and fallen; here is wire; this trench
For months inhabited, twelve times changed hands;
(They soon fall in), used later as a grave.
It has been said on good authority
That in the fighting for this patch of wood
Were killed somewhere above eight thousand men,
Of whom the greater part were buried here,
This mound on which you stand being ...

                          Madame, please,
You are requested kindly not to touch
Or take away the Company's property
As souvenirs; you'll find we have on sale
A large variety, all guaranteed.
As I was saying, all is as it was,
This is an unknown British officer,
The tunic having lately rotted off.
Please follow me – this way ...

the *path*, sir, *please*,
The ground which was secured at great expense
The Company keeps absolutely untouched,
And in that dug-out (genuine) we provide
Refreshments at a reasonable rate.
You are requested not to leave about
Paper, or ginger-beer bottles, or orange-peel,
There are waste-paper baskets at the gate.

G.A. Studdert Kennedy

Dead and Buried

I have borne my cross through Flanders,
  Through the broken heart of France,
I have borne it through the deserts of the East;
  I have wandered, faint and longing,
  Through the human hosts that, thronging,
Swarmed to glut their grinning idols with a feast.

  I was crucified in Cambrai,
    And again outside Bapaume;
I was scourged for miles along the Albert Road,
  I was driven, pierced and bleeding,
  With a million maggots feeding
On the body that I carried as my load.

  I have craved a cup of water,
    Just a drop to quench my thirst,
As the routed armies ran to keep the pace;
  But no soldier made reply
  As the maddened hosts swept by,
And a sweating straggler kicked me in the face.

  There's no ecstasy of torture
    That the devils e'er devised,
That my soul has not endured unto the last;
  As I bore my cross of sorrow,
  For the glory of to-morrow,
Through the wilderness of battles that is past.

  Yet my heart was still unbroken,
    And my hope was still unquenched,
Till I bore my cross to Paris through the crowd.

Soldiers pierced me on the Aisne,
But 'twas by the river Seine
That the statesmen brake my legs and made
my shroud.

There they wrapped my mangled body
In fine linen of fair words,
With the perfume of a sweetly scented lie,
And they laid it in the tomb
Of the golden-mirrored room,
'Mid the many-fountained Gardens of Versailles.

With a thousand scraps of paper
They made fast the open door,
And the wise men of the Council saw it sealed.
With the seal of subtle lying,
They made certain of my dying,
Lest the torment of the peoples should be healed.

Then they set a guard of soldiers
Night and day beside the Tomb,
Where the body of the Prince of Peace is laid,
And the captains of the nations
Keep the sentries to their stations,
Lest the statesman's trust from Satan be betrayed.

For it isn't steel and iron
That men use to kill their God,
But the poison of a smooth and slimy tongue.
Steel and iron tear the body,
But it's oily sham and shoddy
That have trampled down God's *Spirit* in the dung.

G.A. Studdert Kennedy

The Sniper

There's a Jerry over there, Sarge!
Can't you see 'is big square 'ead?
If 'e bobs it up again there,
I'll soon nail 'im – nail 'im dead.
Gimme up that pair o' glasses
And just fix that blinkin' sight,
Gawd! that nearly almost got 'im,
There 'e is now – see? 'Arf right.
If 'e moves again I'll get 'im,
Take these glasses 'ere and see,
What's that? Got 'im through the 'ead, Sarge?
Where's my blarsted cup o' tea?

G.A. Studdert Kennedy

The Spirit

When there ain't no gal to kiss you,
And the postman seems to miss you,
And the fags have skipped an issue,
Carry on.
When ye've got an empty belly,
And the bulley's rotten smelly,
And you're shivering like a jelly,
Carry on.
When the Boche has done your chum in,
And the sergeant's done the rum in,
And there ain't no rations comin',
Carry on.
When the world is red and reeking,
And the shrapnel shells are shrieking,
And your blood is slowly leaking,
Carry on.
When the broken battered trenches,
Are like the bloody butchers' benches,
And the air is thick with stenches,
Carry on.
Carry on,
Though your pals are pale and wan,
And the hope of life is gone,
Carry on.
For to do more than you can,
Is to be a British man,
Not a rotten 'also ran',
Carry on.

G.A. Studdert Kennedy

Waste

Waste of Muscle, waste of Brain,
Waste of Patience, waste of Pain,
Waste of Manhood, waste of Health,
Waste of Beauty, waste of Wealth,
Waste of Blood, and waste of Tears,
Waste of Youth's most precious years,
Waste of ways the Saints have trod,
Waste of Glory, waste of God, –
      War!

G.A. Studdert Kennedy

Woodbine Willie

They gave me this name like their nature,
Compacted of laughter and tears,
A sweet that was born of the bitter,
A joke that was torn from the years

Of their travail and torture, Christ's fools,
Atoning my sins with their blood,
Who grinned in their agony sharing
The glorious madness of God.

Their name! Let me hear it – the symbol
Of unpaid – unpayable debt,
For the men to whom I owed God's Peace,
I put off with a cigarette.

Rudyard Kipling

A Dead Statesman

I could not dig: I dared not rob:
Therefore I lied to please the mob.
Now all my lies are proved untrue
And I must face the men I slew.
What tale shall serve me here among
Mine angry and defrauded young?

Rudyard Kipling

Epitaphs: A Son

My son was killed while laughing at some jest. I
would I knew
What it was, and it might serve me in a time when
jests are few.

Rudyard Kipling

Epitaphs: Common Form

If any question why we died,
Tell them, because our fathers lied.

Rudyard Kipling

For All We Have and Are

For all we have and are,
For all our children's fate,
Stand up and meet the war.
The Hun is at the gate!
Our world has passed away
In wantonness o'erthrown.
There is nothing left today
But steel and fire and stone.

Though all we knew depart,
The old commandments stand:
'In courage keep your heart,
In strength lift up your hand.'

Once more we hear the word
That sickened earth of old:
'No law except the sword
Unsheathed and uncontrolled,'
Once more it knits mankind,
Once more the nations go
To meet and break and bind
A crazed and driven foe.

Comfort, content, delight –
The ages' slow-bought gain –
They shrivelled in a night,
Only ourselves remain
To face the naked days
In silent fortitude,
Through perils and dismays
Renewd and re-renewed.

Though all we made depart,
The old commandments stand:
'In patience keep your heart,
In strength lift up your hand.'

No easy hopes or lies
Shall bring us to our goal,
But iron sacrifice
Of body, will, and soul.
There is but one task for all –
For each one life to give.
Who stands if freedom fall?
Who dies if England live?

Rudyard Kipling

Gethsemane

The Garden called Gethsemane
  In Picardy it was,
And there the people came to see
  The English soldiers pass.
We used to pass – we used to pass
  Or halt, as it might be,
And ship our masks in case of gas
  Beyond Gethsemane.

The Garden called Gethsemane,
  It held a pretty lass,
But all the time she talked to me
  I prayed my cup might pass.
The officer sat on the chair,
  The men lay on the grass,
And all the time we halted there
  I prayed my cup might pass –

It didn't pass – it didn't pass –
  It didn't pass from me.
I drank it when we met the gas
  Beyond Gethsemane.

Rudyard Kipling

My Boy Jack

'Have you news of my boy Jack?'
   Not this tide.
'When d'you think that he'll come back?'
   Not with this wind blowing, and this tide.

'Has any one else had word of him?'
   Not this tide.
For what is sunk will hardly swim,
   Not with this wind blowing, and this tide.

'Oh, dear, what comfort can I find?'
   None this tide,
   Nor any tide,
Except he did not shame his kind –
   Not even with that wind blowing, and that tide.

Then hold your head up all the more,
   This tide,
   And every tide;
Because he was the son you bore,
   And gave to that wind blowing and that tide!

Rudyard Kipling

Epitaphs: The Coward

I could not look on Death, which being known,
Men led me to him, blindfold and alone.

Winifred M. Letts

The Deserter

There was a man – don't mind his name,
Whom Fear had dogged by night and day.
He could not face the German guns
And so he turned and ran away.
Just that – he turned and ran away,
But who can judge him, you or I?
God makes a man of flesh and blood
Who yearns to live and not to die.
And this man when he feared to die
Was scared as any frightened child,
His knees were shaking under him,
His breath came fast, his eyes were wild.
I've seen a hare with eyes as wild,
With throbbing heart and sobbing breath.
But oh! it shames one's soul to see
A man in abject fear of death.

But fear had gripped him, so had death;
His number had gone up that day,
They might not heed his frightened eyes,
They shot him when the dawn was grey.
Blindfolded, when the dawn was grey,
He stood there in a place apart,
The shots rang out and down he fell,
An English bullet in his heart.
An English bullet in his heart!
But here's the irony of life –
His mother thinks he fought and fell
A hero, foremost in the strife.
So she goes proudly; to the strife
Her best, her hero son she gave.
O well for her she does not know
He lies in a deserter's grave.

W.S.S. Lyon

I Tracked a Dead Man Down a Trench

I tracked a dead man down a trench,
    I knew not he was dead.
They told me he had gone that way,
    And there his foot-marks led.

The trench was long and close and curved,
    It seemed without an end;
And as I threaded each new bay
    I thought to see my friend.

I went there stooping to the ground.
    For, should I raise my head,
Death watched to spring; and how should then
    A dead man find the dead?

At last I saw his back. He crouched
    As still as still could be,
And when I called his name aloud
    He did not answer me.

The floor-way of the trench was wet
    Where he was crouching dead:
The water of the pool was brown,
    And round him it was red.

I stole up softly where he stayed
   With head hung down all slack,
And on his shoulders laid my hands
   And drew him gently back.

And then, as I had guessed, I saw
   His head, and how the crown –
I saw then why he crouched so still,
   And why his head hung down.

W.S.S. Lyon

Lines Written in a Fire Trench

'Tis midnight, and above the hollow trench
Seen through a gaunt wood's battle-blasted trunks
And the stark rafters of a shattered grange,
The quiet sky hangs huge and thick with stars.
And through the vast gloom, murdering its peace,
Guns bellow and their shells rush swishing ere
They burst in death and thunder, or they fling
Wild jangling spirals round the screaming air.
Bullets whine by, and maxims drub like drums,
And through the heaped confusion of all sounds
One great gun drives its single vibrant 'Broum'.
And scarce five score of paces from the wall
Of piled sand-bags and barb-toothed nets of wire
(So near and yet what thousand leagues away)
The unseen foe both adds and listens to
The selfsame discord, eyed by the same stars.
Deep darkness hides the desolated land,
Save where a sudden flare sails up and bursts
In whitest glare above the wilderness,
And for one instant lights with lurid pallor
The tense, packed faces in the black redoubt.

Ewart Alan Mackintosh

Before the Summer

When our men are marching lightly up and down,
When the pipes are playing through the little town,
I see a thin line swaying through wind and mud and
    rain
And the broken regiments come back to rest again.

Now the pipes are playing, now the drums are beat,
Now the strong battalions are marching up the
    street.
But the pipes will not be playing and the bayonets
    will not shine.
When the regiments I dream of come stumbling
    down the line.

Between the battered trenches their silent dead will
    lie
Quiet with grave eyes staring at the summer sky.
There is a mist upon them so that I cannot see
The faces of my friends that walk the little town
    with me.

Lest we see a worse thing than it is to die.
Live ourselves and see our friends cold beneath the
    sky,
God grant we too be lying there in wind and mud
    and rain
Before the broken regiments come stumbling back
    again.

Corbie, 1916

Ewart Alan Mackintosh

Ghosts of War

When you and I are buried
With grasses over head,
The memory of our fights will stand
Above this bare and tortured land,
We knew ere we were dead.

Though grasses grow on Vimy,
And poppies at Messines,
And in High Wood the children play,
The craters and the graves will stay
To show what things have been.

Though all be quiet in day-time,
The night shall bring a change,
And peasants walking home shall see
Shell-torn meadow and riven tree,
And their own fields grown strange.

They shall hear live men crying,
They shall see dead men lie,
Shall hear the rattling Maxims fire,
And see by broken twists of wire
Gold flares light up the sky.

And in their new-built houses
The frightened folk will see
Pale bombers coming down the street,
And hear the flurry of charging feet,
And the crash of Victory.

This is our Earth baptized
With the red wine of War.
Horror and courage hand in hand
Shall brood upon the stricken land
In silence evermore.

Ewart Alan Mackintosh

In Memoriam

So you were David's father,
And he was your only son,
And the new-cut peats are rotting
And the work is left undone,
Because of an old man weeping,
Just an old man in pain,
For David, his son David,
That will not come again.

Oh, the letters he wrote you,
And I can see them still,
Not a word of the fighting,
But just the sheep on the hill
And how you should get the crops in
Ere the year get stormier,
And the Bosches have got his body,
And I was his officer.

You were only David's father,
But I had fifty sons
When we went up in the evening
Under the arch of the guns,
And we came back at twilight –
O God! I heard them call
To me for help and pity
That could not help at all.

Oh, never will I forget you,
My men that trusted me,
More my sons than your fathers',
For they could only see
The little helpless babies
And the young men in their pride.
They could not see you dying,
And hold you while you died.

Happy and young and gallant,
They saw their first-born go,
But not the strong limbs broken
And the beautiful men brought low,
The piteous writhing bodies,
They screamed 'Don't leave me, sir,'
For they were only your fathers
But I was your officer.

Ewart Alan Mackintosh

Recruiting

'Lads, you're wanted, go and help,'
On the railway carriage wall
Stuck the poster, and I thought
Of the hands that penned the call.

Fat civilians wishing they
'Could go and fight the Hun.'
Can't you see them thanking God
That they're over forty-one?

Girls with feathers, vulgar songs –
Washy verse on England's need –
God – and don't we damned well know
How the message ought to read.

'Lads, you're wanted! over there,
Shiver in the morning dew,
More poor devils like yourselves
Waiting to be killed by you.

Go and help to swell the names
In the casualty lists.
Help to make the column's stuff
For the blasted journalists.

Help to keep them nice and safe
From the wicked German foe.
Don't let him come over here!
Lads, you're wanted – out you go.'

There's a better word than that,
Lads, and can't you hear it come
From a million men that call
You to share their martyrdom?

Leave the harlots still to sing
Comic songs about the Hun,
Leave the fat old men to say
Now *we've* got them on the run.

Better twenty honest years
Than their dull three score and ten.
Lads, you're wanted. Come and learn
To live and die with honest men.

You shall learn what men can do
If you will but pay the price,
Learn the gaity and strength
In the gallant sacrifice.
Take your risk of life and death
Underneath the open sky.
Live clean or go out quick –
Lads, you're wanted. Come and die.

Ewart Alan Mackintosh

Sniper Sandy

To the Tune: Sister Susie's sewing shirts for soldiers.

Sandy Mac the sniper is a-sniping from his loop-
    hole,
With a telescopic rifle he is looking for a Hun.
If he sees a sniper lurking, or a working-party
    working,
At once he opens fire on them, and bags them every
    one.
And when you come into our trench, by night-time
    or by day.
We take you to his loop-hole, and we point to him
    and say –

Chorus –
'Sniper Sandy's slaying Saxon soldiers,
And Saxon soldiers seldom show but Sandy slays a
    few,
And every day the Bosches put up little wooden
    crosses
In the cemetery for Saxon soldiers Sniper Sandy slew.'

Now in the German trenches there's a sniper they
    call Hermann,
A stout and stolid Saxon with a healthy growth of
    beard,
And Hermann with his rifle is the pride of every
    German,
Until our Sandy gets on him, and Hermann gets
    afeared,

For when he hears the bullets come he slides down
    to the ground,
And trembling he gasps out to his comrades all
    around –

Chorus –
'Sniper Sandy's slaying Saxon soldiers,
And Saxon soldiers seldom show but Sandy slays a
    few,
And every day the Bosches put up little wooden
    crosses
In the cemetery for Saxon soldiers Sniper Sandy slew.'

The Seaforths got so proud of Sandy's prowess with
    his rifle,
They drew up a report on him and sent it to the
    Corps,
And ninety-seven was his bag – it doesn't seem a
    trifle –
But Sandy isn't certain that it wasn't rather more,
And when Sir John French heard of it, he broke into
    a laugh,
And rubbed his hands and chuckled to the Chief of
    General Staff –

Chorus –
'Sniper Sandy's slaying Saxon soldiers,
And Saxon soldiers seldom show but Sandy slays a
    few,
And every day the Bosches put up little wooden
    crosses
In the cemetery for Saxon soldiers Sniper Sandy slew.'

Ewart Alan Mackintosh

To My Sister

If I die to-morrow
I shall go happily.
With the flush of battle on my face
I shall walk with an eager pace
The road I cannot see.

My life burnt fiercely always,
And fiercely will go out
With glad wild fighting ringed around.
But you will be above the ground
And darkness all about.

You will not hear the shouting.
You will not see the pride,
Only with tortured memory
Remember what I used to be,
And dream of how I died.

You will see gloom and horror
But never the joy of fight.
You'll dream of me in pain and fear,
And in your dreaming never hear
My voice across the night.

My voice that sounds so gaily
Will be too far away
For you to see across your dream
The charging and the bayonet's gleam,
Or hear the words I say.

And parted by the warders
That hold the gates of sleep,
I shall be dead and happy
And you will live and weep.

John McCrae

In Flanders Fields

In Flanders fields the poppies blow
Between the crosses, row on row
    That mark our place; and in the sky
    The larks, still bravely singing, fly
Scarce heard amid the guns below.

We are the Dead. Short days ago
We lived, felt dawn, saw sunset glow,
    Loved and were loved, and now we lie
        In Flanders fields.

Take up our quarrel with the foe:
To you from failing hands we throw
    The torch; be yours to hold it high.
    If ye break faith with us who die
We shall not sleep, though poppies grow
        In Flanders fields.

A.J. Mann

The Shell Hole

In the Shell Hole he lies, this German soldier of a
    year ago;
But he is not as then, accoutred, well, and eager for
    the foe
He hoped so soon, so utterly, to crush. His muddy
    skull
Lies near the mangled remnants of his corpse – war's
    furies thus annul
The pomp and pageantry that were its own. White
    rigid bones
Gape through the nauseous chaos of his clothes; the
    cruel stones
Hold fast the letter he was wont to clasp close to his
    am'rous breast.
Here 'neath the stark, keen stars, where is no peace,
    no joy, nor any rest,
He lies. There, to the right, his boot, gashed by the
    great shell's fiendish whim,
Retains – O horrid spectacle! – the fleshless stump
    that was his limb!
Vile rats and mice, and flies and lice and ghastly
    things that carrion know
Have made a travesty of Death of him who lived a
    year ago.

A.J. Mann

The Soldier

'Tis strange to look on a man that is dead
As he lies in the shell-swept hell,
And to think that the poor black battered corpse
Once lived like you and was well.

'Tis stranger far when you come to think
That you may be soon like him …
And it's Fear that tugs at your trembling soul,
A Fear that is weird and grim!

Frederick Manning

Grotesque

These are the damned circles Dante trod,
Terrible in hopelessness,
But even skulls have their humour,
An eyeless and sardonic mockery:
And we,
Sitting with streaming eyes in the acrid smoke,
That murks our foul, damp billet,
Chant bitterly, with raucous voices
As a choir of frogs
In hideous irony, our patriotic songs.

John Masefield

August 1914

How still this quiet cornfield is to-night!
By an intenser glow the evening falls,
Bringing, not darkness, but a deeper light;
Among the stooks a partridge covey calls.

The windows glitter on the distant hill;
Beyond the hedge the sheep-bells in the fold
Stumble on sudden music and are still;
The forlorn pinewoods droop above the wold.

An endless quiet valley reaches out
Past the blue hills into the evening sky;
Over the stubble, cawing, goes a rout
Of rooks from harvest, flagging as they fly.

So beautiful it is, I never saw
So great a beauty on these English fields,
Touched by the twilight's coming into awe,
Ripe to the soul and rich with summer's yields.

* * *

These homes, this valley spread below me here,
The rooks, the tilted stacks, the beasts in pen,
Have been the heartfelt things, past-speaking dear
To unknown generations of dead men,

Who, century after century, held these farms,
And, looking out to watch the changing sky,
Heard, as we hear, the rumours and alarms
Of war at hand and danger pressing nigh.

133

And knew, as we know, that the message meant
The breaking off of ties, the loss of friends,
Death, like a miser getting in his rent,
And no new stones laid where the trackway ends.

The harvest not yet won, the empty bin,
The friendly horses taken from the stalls,
The fallow on the hill not yet brought in,
The cracks unplastered in the leaking walls.

Yet heard the news, and went discouraged home,
And brooded by the fire with heavy mind,
With such dumb loving of the Berkshire loam
As breaks the dumb hearts of the English kind,

Then sadly rose and left the well-loved Downs,
And so by ship to sea, and knew no more
The fields of home, the byres, the market towns,
Nor the dear outline of the English shore,

But knew the misery of the soaking trench,
The freezing in the rigging, the despair
In the revolting second of the wrench
When the blind soul is flung upon the air,

And died (uncouthly, most) in foreign lands
For some idea but dimly understood
Of an English city never built by hands
Which love of England prompted and made good.

* * *

If there be any life beyond the grave,
It must be near the men and things we love,
Some power of quick suggestion how to save,
Touching the living soul as from above.

An influence from the Earth from those dead hearts
So passionate once, so deep, so truly kind,
That in the living child the spirit starts,
Feeling companioned still, not left behind.

Surely above these fields a spirit broods
A sense of many watchers muttering near
Of the lone Downland with the forlorn woods
Loved to the death, inestimably dear.

A muttering from beyond the veils of Death
From long-dead men, to whom this quiet scene
Came among blinding tears with the last breath,
The dying soldier's vision of his queen.

All the unspoken worship of those lives
Spent in forgotten wars at other calls
Glimmers upon these fields where evening drives
Beauty like breath, so gently darkness falls.

Darkness that makes the meadows holier still,
The elm-trees sadden in the hedge, a sigh
Moves in the beech-clump on the haunted hill,
The rising planets deepen in the sky,

And silence broods like spirit on the brae,
A glimmering moon begins, the moonlight runs
Over the grasses of the ancient way
Rutted this morning by the passing guns.

Charlotte Mew

The Cenotaph

Not yet will those measureless fields be green again
Where only yesterday the wild sweet blood
     of wonderful youth was shed;
There is a grave whose earth must hold too long,
      too deep a stain,
Though for ever over it we may speak
     as proudly as we may tread.
But here, where the watchers by lonely hearths from
 the thrust of an inward sword have more slowly
  bled,
We shall build the Cenotaph: Victory, winged,
   with Peace, winged too, at the column's head.
And over the stairway, at the foot – oh! here,
   leave desolate, passionate hands to spread
Violets, roses, and laurel, with the small, sweet,
     tinkling country things
Speaking so wistfully of other Springs,
From the little gardens of little places
  where son or sweetheart was born and bred.
In splendid sleep, with a thousand brothers
To lovers – to mothers
Here, too, lies he:
Under the purple, the green, the red,
It is all young life: it must break
     some women's hearts to see
Such a brave, gay coverlet to such a bed!
Only, when all is done and said,
God is not mocked and neither are the dead.

For this will stand in our Marketplace –
Who'll sell, who'll buy
(Will you or I
Lie each to each with the better grace)?
While looking into every busy whore's
                         and huckster's face
As they drive their bargains, is the Face
Of God: and some young, piteous, murdered face.

Vincent Morris

The Eleventh Hour

A Sonnet

Is this to live? – to cower and stand aside
   While others fight and perish day by day?
   To see my loved ones slaughtered, and to say: –
'Bravo! bravo! how nobly you have died!'
Is this to love? – to heed my friends no more,
   But watch them perish in a foreign land
   Unheeded, and to give no helping hand,
But smile, and say: – 'How terrible is War!'

Nay: this is not to love nor this to live!
I will go forth; I hold no more aloof;
And I will give all that I have to give
And leave the refuge of my father's roof:

Then, if I live, no man will say, think I,
'He lives: because he did not dare to die!'

Sir Henry Newbolt

A Letter from the Front

I was out early today, spying about
From the top of a haystack – such a lovely morning –
And when I mounted again to canter back
I saw across a field in the broad sunlight
A young Gunner Subaltern, stalking along
With a rook-rifle held at the ready, and – would you
    believe it? –
A domestic cat, soberly marching beside him.

So I laughed, and felt quite well disposed to the
    youngster,
And shouted out 'the top of the morning' to him,
And wished him 'Good sport!' – and then I
    remembered
My rank, and his, and what I ought to be doing:
And I rode nearer, and added, 'I can only suppose
You have not seen the Commander-in-Chief's order
Forbidding English officers to annoy their Allies
By hunting and shooting.'
                But he stood and saluted
And said earnestly, 'I beg your pardon, Sir,
I was only going out to shoot a sparrow
To feed my cat with.'

So there was the whole picture,
The lovely early morning, the occasional shell
Screeching and scattering past us, the empty
    landscape, –
Empty, except for the young Gunner saluting,
And the cat, anxiously watching his every
    movement.

I may be wrong, and I may have told it badly,
But it struck *me* as being extremely ludicrous.

Sir Henry Newbolt

Clifton Chapel

This is the Chapel: here, my son,
Your father thought the thoughts of youth,
And heard the words that one by one
The touch of life has turned to truth.
Here in a day that is not far
You too may speak with noble ghosts
Of manhood and the vows of war
You made before the Lord of Hosts.

To set the cause above renown,
To love the game beyond the prize,
To honour, while you strike him down,
The foe that comes with fearless eyes;
To count the life of battle good,
And dear the land that gave you birth,
And dearer yet the brotherhood
That binds the brave of all the earth.

My son, the oath is yours: the end
Is His, who built the world for strife,
Who gave His children pain for friend,
And death for surest hope of life.
Today and here the fight's begun,
Of the great fellowship you're free;
Henceforth the school and you are one,
And what you are, the race shall be.

God send you fortune, yet be sure,
Among the lights that gleam and pass,
You'll live to follow none more pure
Than that which glows on yonder brass:
'*Qui procul hinc,*' the legend's writ, –
The frontier-grave is far away –
'*Qui ante diem periit:*
Sed miles, sed pro patria.'

Robert Nichols

Casualty

They are bringing him down,
He looks at me wanly.
The bandages are brown,
Brown with mud, red only –
But how deep a red! in the breast of the shirt,
Deepening red too, as each whistling breath
Is drawn with the suck of a slow-filling squirt
While waxen cheeks waste to the pallor of death.

O my comrade!
My comrade that you could rest
Your tired body on mine, that your head might be
    laid
Fallen and heavy – upon this my breast,
That I might take your hands in my hands
To chafe! That abandoned your body might sink
Upon mine, which here helplessly, grievously stands;
That your body might drink
Warmth from my body, strength from my veins,
Life from my heart that monstrously beats,
Beats, beats and strains
After you vainly!
The trench curves. They are gone.
The steep rain teems down.

O my companion!
Who were you? How did you come,
Looking so wanly upon me? I know –
And O, how immensely long I have known –
Those aching eyes, numb face, gradual gloom,
That depth without groan!
Take now my love – this love which alone
I can give you – and shed without pain –
That life if I could I would succour,
Even as it were
This, this, my poor own!

Robert Nichols

Eve of Assault:
Infantry Going Down to Trenches

Downward slopes the wild red sun.
We lie around a waiting gun;
Soon we shall load and fire and load.
But, hark! a sound beats down the road.

' 'Ello! wot's up?'
'Let's 'ave a look!' 'Come on, Ginger, drop that book!'
'Wot an 'ell of bloody noise!'
'It's the Yorks and Lancs, meboys!'

So we crowd: hear, watch them come –
One man drubbing on a drum,
A crazy, high mouth-organ blowing,
Tin cans rattling, cat-calls, crowing …

And above their rhythmic feet
A whirl of shrilling loud and sweet,
Round mouths whistling in unison;
Shouts: ' 'O's goin' to out the 'Un?

'Back us up, mates!' 'Gawd, we will!'
' 'Eave them shells at Kaiser Bill!'
'Art from Lancashire, melad?'
'Gi' 'en a cheer, boys; make 'en glad.'

' 'Ip 'urrah!' 'Give Fritz the chuck.'
'Good ol' bloody Yorks!' 'Good-luck!'
'Cheer!'
I cannot cheer or speak
Lest my voice, my heart must break.

Robert Nichols

The Approach

1.   *In the Grass: Halt by the Wayside*

In my tired, helpless body
I feel my sunk heart ache;
But suddenly, loudly
The far, the great guns shake.

Is it sudden terror
Burdens my heart? My hand
Flies to my head. I listen …
And do not understand.

Is death so near, then?
From this blazing light,
Do I plunge suddenly
Into vortex? Night?

Guns again! the quiet
Shakes at the vengeful voice …
It is terrible pleasure
I do not fear; I rejoice.

2.   *On the Way Up*

The battery grides and jingles,
Mile succeeds to mile;
Shaking the noonday sunshine,
The guns lunge out a while
And then are still a while.

We amble along the highway;
The reeking, powdery dust
Ascends and cakes our faces,
With a striped, sweaty crust.

Under the still sky's violet
The heat throbs in the air …
The white road's dusty radiance,
Assumes a dark glare.

With a head hot and heavy,
And eyes that cannot rest,
And a black heart burning
In a stifled breast,

I sit in the saddle,
I feel the road unroll,
And keep my senses straightened
Toward to-morrow's goal.

There over unknown meadows,
Which we must reach at last,
Day and night thunders
A black and chilly blast.

Heads forget heaviness,
Hearts forget spleen,
For by that mighty winnowing
Being is blown clean.

Light in the eyes again,
Strength in the hand,
A spirit dares, dies, forgives
And can understand.

And best! Love comes back again
After grief and shame,
And along the wind of death
Throws a clean flame!

The battery grides and jingles;
Mile succeeds to mile;
Suddenly battering the silence
The guns burst out a while.

I lift my head and smile.

3. *Nearer*

Nearer and ever nearer ...
My body tired but tense
Hovers 'twixt vague pleasure
And tremulous confidence.

Arms to have and to use them,
And a soul to be made
Worthy if not worthy;
If afraid, unafraid!

To endure for a little.
To endure and have done:
Men I love about me,
Over me the sun!

And should at last suddenly
Fly the speeding death:
The four great quarters of heaven
Receive this little breath.

Wilfred Owen

Anthem for Doomed Youth

What passing bells for those who die as cattle?
    Only the monstrous anger of the guns.
    Only the stuttering rifles' rapid rattle
Can patter out their hasty orisons.
No mockeries for them from prayers or bells,
    Nor any voice of mourning save the choirs, –
The shrill, demented choirs of wailing shells;
    And bugles calling for them from sad shires.
What candles may be held to speed them all?
    Not in the hands of boys, but in their eyes
Shall shine the holy glimmers of good-byes.
    The pallor of girls' brows shall be their pall;
Their flowers the tenderness of patient minds,
And each slow dusk a drawing-down of blinds.

Wilfred Owen

Apologia pro Poemate Meo

I, too, saw God through mud –
    The mud that cracked on cheeks when wretches
      smiled.
    War brought more glory to their eyes than
      blood,
    And gave their laughs more glee than shakes a
      child.

Merry it was to laugh there –
    Where death becomes absurd and life absurder.
    For power was on us as we slashed bones bare
    Not to feel sickness or remorse of murder.

I, too, have dropped off fear –
    Behind the barrage, dead as my platoon,
    And sailed my spirit surging, light and clear,
    Past the entanglement where hopes lay strewn;

And witnessed exhultation –
    Faces that used to curse me, scowl for scowl,
    Shine and lift up with passion of oblation,
    Seraphic for an hour, though they were foul.

I have made fellowships –
    Untold of happy lovers in old song.
    For love is not the binding of fair lips
    With the soft silk of eyes that look and long,

By Joy, whose ribbon slips, –
    But wound with war's hard wire whose stakes
      are strong;
    Bound with the bandage of the arm that drips;
    Knit in the welding of the rifle-thong.

I have perceived much beauty
    In the hoarse oaths that kept our courage
      straight;
    Heard music in the silentness of duty;
    Found peace where shell-storms spouted
      reddest spate.

Nevertheless, except you share
    With them in hell the sorrowful dark of hell,
    Whose world is but a trembling of a flare
    And heaven but a highway for a shell,

You shall not hear their mirth:
    You shall not come to think them well content
    By any jest of mine. These men are worth
    Your tears: You are not worth their merriment.

Wilfred Owen

Asleep

Under his helmet, up against his pack,
After the many days of work and waking,
Sleep took him by the brow and laid him back.
And in the happy no-time of his sleeping,
Death took him by the heart. There was a quaking
Of the aborted life within him leaping ...
Then chest and sleepy arms once more fell slack.
And soon the slow, stray blood came creeping
From the intrusive lead, like ants on track.

* * *

Whether his deeper sleep lie shaded by the shaking
Of great wings, and the thoughts that hung the stars,
High pillowed on calm pillows of God's making
Above these clouds, these rains, these sleets of lead,
And these winds' scimitars;
– Or whether yet his thin and sodden head
Confuses more and more with the low mould,
His hair being one with the grey grass
And finished fields of autumns that are old ...
Who knows? Who hopes? Who troubles? Let it
    pass!
He sleeps. He sleeps less tremulous, less cold
Than we who must awake, and waking, say Alas!

Wilfred Owen

Disabled

He sat in a wheeled chair, waiting for dark,
And shivered in his ghastly suit of grey,
Legless, sewn short at elbow. Through the park
Voices of boys rang saddening like a hymn,
Voices of play and pleasure after day,
Till gathering sleep had mothered them from him.

About this time Town used to swing so gay
When glow-lamps budded in the light-blue trees
And girls glanced lovelier as the air grew dim,
– In the old times, before he threw away his knees.
Now he will never feel again how slim
Girls' waists are, or how warm their subtle hands,
All of them touch him like some queer disease.

There was an artist silly for his face,
For it was younger than his youth, last year.
Now he is old; his back will never brace;
He's lost his colour very far from here,
Poured it down shell-holes till the veins ran dry,
And half his lifetime lapsed in the hot race,
And leap of purple spurted from his thigh.
One time he liked a bloodsmear down his leg,
After the matches carried shoulder-high.
It was after football, when he'd drunk a peg,
He thought he'd better join. He wonders why …
Someone had said he'd look a god in kilts.

That's why; and maybe, too, to please his Meg,
Aye, that was it, to please the giddy jilts,
He asked to join. He didn't have to beg;
Smiling they wrote his lie; aged nineteen years.
Germans he scarcely thought of; and no fears
Of Fear came yet. He thought of jewelled hilts
For daggers in plaid socks; of smart salutes;
And care of arms; and leave; and pay arrears;
Esprit de corps; and hints for young recruits.
And soon, he was drafted out with drums and
     cheers.

Some cheered him home, but not as crowds cheer
     Goal.
Only a solemn man who brought him fruits
Thanked him; and then inquired about his soul.
Now, he will spend a few sick years in Institutes,
And do what things the rules consider wise,
And take whatever pity they may dole.
To-night he noticed how the women's eyes
Passed from him to the strong men that were whole.
How cold and late it is! Why don't they come
And put him into bed? Why don't they come?

Wilfred Owen

Dulce et Decorum est

Bent double, like old beggars under sacks,
Knock-kneed, coughing like hags, we cursed through
    sludge,
Till on the haunting flares we turned our backs,
And towards our distant rest began to trudge.
Men marched asleep. Many had lost their boots,
But limped on, blood-shod. All went lame, all blind;
Drunk with fatigue; deaf even to the hoots
Of gas-shells dropping softly behind.

Gas! Gas! Quick, boys! – An ecstasy of fumbling,
Fitting the clumsy helmets just in time,
But someone still was yelling out and stumbling
And floundering like a man in fire or lime. –
Dim through the misty panes and thick green light,
As under a green sea, I saw him drowning.
In all my dreams, before my helpless sight,
He plunges at me, guttering, choking, drowning.

If in some smothering dreams, you too could pace
Behind the wagon that we flung him in,
And watch the white eyes writhing in his face,
His hanging face, like a devil's sick of sin;
If you could hear, at every jolt, the blood
Come gargling from the froth-corrupted lungs,
Obscene as cancer, bitter as the cud
Of vile, incurable sores on innocent tongues, –
My friend, you would not tell with such high zest
To children ardent for some desperate glory,
The old Lie: *Dulce et decorum est*
Pro patria mori.

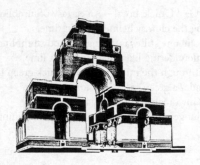

Wilfred Owen

Exposure

I

Our brains ache, in the merciless iced east winds that
    knife us …
Wearied we keep awake because the night is silent …
Low drooping flares confuse our memory of the
    salient …
Worried by silence, sentries whisper, curious,
    nervous,
  But nothing happens.

Watching, we hear the mad gusts tugging on the
    wire,
Like twitching agonies of men among its brambles.
Northward incessantly, the flickering gunnery
    rumbles,
Far off, like a dull rumour of some other war.
  What are we doing here?

The poignant misery of dawn begins to grow …
We only know war lasts, rain soaks, and clouds sag
    stormy.
Dawn massing in the east her melancholy army
Attacks once more in ranks on shivering ranks of
    grey,
  But nothing happens.

Sudden successive flights of bullets streak the silence.
Less deadly than the air that shudders black with
    snow,
With sidelong flowing flakes that flock, pause, and
    renew,
We watch them wandering up and down the wind's
    nonchalance,
  But nothing happens.

II

Pale flakes with fingering stealth come feeling for
    our faces –
We cringe in holes, back on forgotten dreams, and
    stare, snow-dazed,
Deep into grassier ditches. So we drowse, sun-dozed,
Littered with blossoms trickling where the blackbird
    fusses.
  Is it that we are dying?

Slowly our ghosts drag home: glimpsing the sunk
    fires, glozed
With crusted dark-red jewels; crickets jingle there;
For hours the innocent mice rejoice: the house is
    theirs;
Shutters and doors all closed: on us the doors are
    closed –
  We turn back to our dying.

Since we believe not otherwise can kind fires burn;
Nor ever suns smile true on child, or field, or fruit.
For God's invincible spring our love is made afraid;
Therefore, not loath, we lie out here; therefore were
　　born,
　　For love of God seems dying.

Tonight, His frost will fasten on this mud and us,
Shrivelling many hands and puckering foreheads
　　crisp.
The burying party, picks and shovels in their shaking
　　grasp,
Pause over half-known faces. All their eyes are ice,
　　But nothing happens.

Wilfred Owen

Futility

Move him into the sun –
Gently its touch awoke him once,
At home, whispering of fields unsown.
Always it woke him, even in France,
Until this morning and this snow.
If anything might rouse him now
The kind old sun will know.

Think how it wakes the seeds, –
Woke, once, the clays of a cold star.
Are limbs, so dear-achieved, are sides,
Full-nerved, – still warm, – too hard to stir?
Was it for this the clay grew tall?
– O what made fatuous sunbeams toil
To break earth's sleep at all?

Wilfred Owen

Greater Love

Red lips are not so red
As the stained stones kissed by the English dead.
Kindness of wooed and wooer
Seems shame to their love pure.
O Love, your eyes lose lure
When I behold eyes blinded in my stead!

Your slender attitude
Trembles not exquisite like limbs knife-skewed,
Rolling and rolling there
Where God seems not to care;
Till the fierce Love they bear
Cramps them in death's extreme decrepitude.

Your voice sings not so soft, –
Though even as wind murmuring through raftered
    loft, –
Your dear voice is not dear,
Gentle, and evening clear,
As theirs whom none now hear
Now earth has stopped their piteous mouths that
    coughed.

Heart, you were never hot,
Nor large, nor full like hearts made great with shot;
And though your hand be pale,
Paler are all which trail
Your cross through flame and hail:
Weep, you may weep, for you may touch them not.

Wilfred Owen

Insensibility

I

Happy are men who yet before they are killed
Can let their veins run cold.
Whom no compassion fleers
Or makes their feet
Sore on the alleys cobbled with their brothers.
The front line withers,
But they are troops who fade, not flowers
For poets' tearful fooling:
Men, gaps for filling
Losses who might have fought
Longer; but no one bothers.

II

And some cease feeling
Even themselves or for themselves.
Dullness best solves
The tease and doubt of shelling,
And Chance's strange arithmetic
Comes simpler than the reckoning of their shilling.
They keep no check on Armies' decimation.

III

Happy are these who lose imagination:
They have enough to carry with ammunition.
Their spirit drags no pack.
Their old wounds save with cold can not more ache.
Having seen all things red,
Their eyes are rid
Of the hurt of the colour of blood for ever.
And terror's first constriction over,
Their hearts remain small drawn.
Their senses in some scorching cautery of battle
Now long since ironed,
Can laugh among the dying, unconcerned.

IV

Happy the soldier home, with not a notion
How somewhere, every dawn, some men attack,
And many sighs are drained.
Happy the lad whose mind was never trained:
His days are worth forgetting more than not.
He sings along the march
Which we march taciturn, because of dusk,
The long, forlorn, relentless trend
From larger day to huger night.

V

We wise, who with a thought besmirch
Blood over all our soul,
How should we see our task
But through his blunt and lashless eyes?
Alive, he is not vital overmuch;
Dying, not mortal overmuch;
Nor sad, nor proud,
Nor curious at all.
He cannot tell
Old men's placidity from his.

IV

But cursed are dullards whom no cannon stuns,
That they should be as stones.
Wretched are they, and mean
With paucity that never was simplicity.
By choice they made themselves immune
To pity and whatever mourns in man
Before the last sea and the hapless stars;
Whatever mourns when many leave these shores;
Whatever shares
The eternal reciprocity of tears.

Wilfred Owen

Inspection

'You! What d'you mean by this?' I rapped.
'You dare come on parade like this?'
'Please, sir, it's –' ''Old yer mouth,' the sergeant
    snapped.
'I takes 'is name, sir?' – 'Please, and then dismiss.'

Some days 'confined to camp' he got,
For being 'dirty on parade'.
He told me, afterwards, the damned spot
Was blood, his own. 'Well, blood is dirt,' I said.

'Blood's dirt,' he laughed, looking away
Far off to where his wound had bled
And almost merged for ever into clay.
'The world is washing out its stains,' he said.
'It doesn't like our cheeks so red:
Young blood's its great objection.
But when we're duly white-washed, being dead,
The race will bear Field-Marshal God's inspection.'

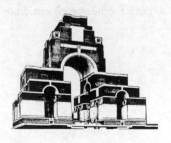

Wilfred Owen

Mental Cases

Who are these? Why sit they here in twilight?
Wherefore rock they, purgatorial shadows,
Drooping tongues from jaws that slob their relish,
Baring teeth that leer like skulls' tongues wicked?
Stroke on stroke of pain, – but what slow panic,
Gouged these chasms round their fretted sockets?
Ever from their hair and through their hand palms
Misery swelters. Surely we have perished
Sleeping, and walk hell; but who these hellish?

– These are men whose minds the Dead have
        ravished.
Memory fingers in their hair of murders,
Multitudinous murders they once witnessed.
Wading sloughs of flesh these helpless wander,
Treading blood from lungs that had loved laughter.
Always they must see these things and hear them,
Batter of guns and shatter of flying muscles,
Carnage incomparable and human squander
Rucked too thick for these men's extrication.

Therefore still their eyeballs shrink tormented
Back into their brains, because on their sense
Sunlight seems a bloodsmear; night comes blood-
    black;
Dawn breaks open like a wound that bleeds afresh
– Thus their heads wear this hilarious, hideous,
Awful falseness of set-smiling corpses.
– Thus their hands are plucking at each other;
Picking at the rope-knouts of their scourging;
Snatching after us who smote them, brother,
Pawing us who dealt them war and madness.

Wilfred Owen

Strange Meeting

It seemed that out of battle I escaped
Down some profound dull tunnel, long since
    scooped
Through granites which titanic wars had groined.

Yet also there encumbered sleepers groaned,
Too fast in thought or death to be bestirred.
Then, as I probed them, one sprang up, and stared
With piteous recognition in fixed eyes,
Lifting distressful hands, as if to bless.
And by his smile, I knew that sullen hall, –
By his dead smile I knew we stood in Hell.

With a thousand pains that vision's face was grained;
Yet no blood reached there from the upper ground,
And no guns thumped, or down the flues made
    moan.
'Strange friend,' I said, 'here is no cause to mourn.'
'None,' said that other, 'save the undone years,
The hopelessness. Whatever hope is yours,
Was my life also; I went hunting wild
After the wildest beauty in the world,
Which lies not calm in eyes, or braided hair,
But mocks the steady running of the hour,
And if it grieves, grieves richlier than here.
For by my glee might many men have laughed,
And of my weeping something had been left,
Which must die now. I mean the truth untold,
The pity of war, the pity war distilled.

Now men will go content with what we spoiled,
Or, discontent, boil bloody, and be spilled.
They will be swift with swiftness of the tigress.
None will break ranks, though nations trek from
    progress.
Courage was mine, and I had mystery,
Wisdom was mine, and I had mastery:
To miss the march of this retreating world
Into vain citadels that are not walled.
Then, when much blood had clogged their chariot-
    wheels,
I would go up and wash them from sweet wells,
Even with truths that lie too deep for taint.
I would have poured my spirit without stint
But not through wounds; not on the cess of war.
Foreheads of men have bled where no wounds were.

I am the enemy you killed, my friend.
I knew you in this dark: for so you frowned
Yesterday through me as you jabbed and killed.
I parried; but my hands were loath and cold.
Let us sleep now …'

Wilfred Owen

The Dead-Beat

He dropped, – more sullenly than wearily,
Lay stupid like a cod, heavy like meat,
And none of us could kick him to his feet;
Just blinked at my revolver, blearily;
– Didn't appear to know a war was on,
Or see the blasted trench at which he stared.
'I'll do 'em in,' he whined, 'If this hand's spared,
I'll murder them, I will.'

A low voice said,
'It's Blighty, p'raps, he sees; his pluck's all gone,
Dreaming of all the valiant, that AREN'T dead:
Bold uncles, smiling ministerially;
Maybe his brave young wife, getting her fun
In some new home, improved materially.
It's not these stiffs have crazed him; nor the Hun.'

We sent him down at last, out of the way.
Unwounded; – stout lad, too, before that strafe.
Malingering? Stretcher-bearers winked, 'Not half!'

Next day I heard the Doc's well-whiskied laugh:
'That scum you sent last night soon died. Hooray!'

Wilfred Owen

The Sentry

We'd found an old Boche dug-out, and he knew,
And gave us hell, for shell on frantic shell
Hammered on top, but never quite burst through.
Rain, guttering down in waterfalls of slime
Kept slush waist high, that rising hour by hour,
Choked up the steps too thick with clay to climb.
What murk of air remained stank old, and sour
With fumes of whizz-bangs, and the smell of men
Who'd lived there years, and left their curse in the
     den,
If not their corpses …

               There we herded from the blast
Of whizz-bangs, but one found our door at last.
Buffeting eyes and breath, snuffing the candles.
And thud! flump! thud! down the steep steps came
     thumping
And splashing in the flood, deluging muck –
The sentry's body; then his rifle, handles
Of old Boche bombs, and mud in ruck on ruck.
We dredged him up, for killed, until he whined
'O sir, my eyes – I'm blind – I'm blind, I'm blind!'
Coaxing, I held a flame against his lids
And said if he could see the least blurred light
He was not blind; in time he'd get all right.
'I can't,' he sobbed. Eyeballs, huge-bulged like squids
Watch my dreams still; but I forgot him there
In posting next for duty, and sending a scout
To beg a stretcher somewhere, and floundering about
To other posts under the shrieking air.

Those other wretches, how they bled and spewed,
And one who would have drowned himself for
     good, –
I try not to remember these things now.
Let dread hark back for one word only: how
Half-listening to that sentry's moans and jumps,
And the wild chattering of his broken teeth,
Renewed most horribly whenever crumps
Pummelled the roof and slogged the air beneath –
Through the dense din, I say, we heard him shout
'I see your lights!' But ours had long died out.

Robert Palmer

How Long, O Lord?

How long, O Lord, how long, before the flood
Of crimson-welling carnage shall abate?
From sodden plains in West and East the blood
Of kindly men streams up in mists of hate,
Polluting Thy clean air: and nations great
In reputation of the arts that bind
The world with hopes of Heaven, sink to the state
Of brute barbarians, whose ferocious mind
Gloats o'er the bloody havoc of their kind,
Not knowing love or mercy. Lord, how long
Shall Satan in high places lead the blind
To battle for the passions of the strong?
Oh, touch Thy children's hearts, that they may know
Hate their most hateful, pride their deadliest foe.

Harold Parry

A Sonnet

Deep in the slumbering night hide me away,
Where I may gaze upon unmoving stars,
And feel the scented airs around me play,
Blown from between the golden turned bars
That lie far, far beyond the land of sight,
But not too far beyond the land of sense;
That in the silent starry vaulted night,
The inward soul, across a space immense,
May glimpse the journey's end, and courage take
From vision. So in the searching light of day
Memory may bring a vintage that will slake
My thirst and strengthen me upon the way;
That, though in utter dark, I may not sleep
Whene'er God calls to me across Time's deep.

Vivian Pemberton

An Only Son's Dying Lament

I'm not a soldier born and bred,
I hate the sound of guns,
I joined because they told me
England needed all her sons.

I love old England's country scenes,
The old cliffs by the sea,
The peaceful, mist-clad Devon moors,
'Tis there that I would be.

I love the gentle English girls,
I love their graceful ways,
I love to watch the sheep dog's work,
And the lazy cattle graze.

They used to give me all I asked
In those dear days of old,
They gave me wine, they gave me love,
And never asked for gold.

But now I do not ask for love,
For riches, wine, or song,
They tell me that I'll soon be well,
But I know they are wrong.

A stretcher party brought me here,
My left leg hurt like sin,
They sent my pay-book and my gold
Back to my next of kin.

It is not much for which I ask,
I know my knell has rung,
But they will not give me anything
To cool my burning tongue.

Max Plowman

Going into the Line

At 3.15, No. 11 Platoon, 100 yards in rear of No. 10,
    will move from Pommiers Redoubt.

              So soon!
At 3.15. And would return here ... when?
It didn't say. Who would return? P'raps all,
P'raps none. Then it had come at last!
It had come at last! his own stupendous hour,
Long waited, dreaded, almost hoped-for too,
When all else seemed the foolery of power;
It had come at last! and suddenly the world
Was sharply cut in two. On one side lay
A golden, dreamy, peaceful afternoon,
And on the other, men gone mad with fear,
A hell of noise and darkness, a Last Day
Daily enacted. Now good-bye to one
And to the other ... well, acceptance: that
At least he'd give; many had gone with joy:
He loathed it from his very inmost soul.

The golden world! It lay just over there,
Peacefully dreaming. In its clear bright depths
Friends moved – he saw them going here and
    there,
Like thistledown above an August meadow:
Gently as in a gentle dream they moved,
Unagonized, unwrought, nor sad, nor proud,
Faces he loved to agony – and none
Could see, or know, or bid him well-adieu.
Blasphemous irony! To think how oft

On such a day a friend would hold his hand
Saying good-bye, though they would meet next
    day,
And now … He breathed his whole soul out,
Bidding it span the unbridged senseless miles
And glow about their thoughts in waves of love.

'Twas time already! Now? As soon as this?
Did his voice hold? How did he look to them?
Poor craven little crowd of human mites!
Now they were crawling over the scarred
    cheese,
Silently going towards that roaring sea,
Each thinking his own thought, craving
    perhaps
A body that would fail, or with set teeth
Pitting a human will against the world.
Now every step seemed an eternity:
Each stretch of earth unreachable until it lay
Behind and a stretch longer lay beyond.
Would it never be ended? Crumbling earth,
Dry with the cracks of earthquake, dumbly
    showed
Death had just trodden there – and there he lay,
Foully deformed in what was once a man.
'Lo! as these are, so shalt thou be', he thought,
Shuddered: then thrilled almost to ecstasy,
As one from hell delivered up to heaven.

How slow they moved in front! Yes, slower still.

Then we must stop: we were not eighty yards.
But to stop here – to wait for it! Oh no!
Backward or forward, anything but not stop –
And now he rasps out, 'Halt!' They stand and
    curse,
Eyes furtive, fingers moving senselessly.
There comes a roar nearer and louder till
His head is bursting with noise and the earth
    shakes.
'A bloody near one, that!' and 'What the hell
Are we stuck here for?' come with sudden
    growls.
He moves without a word, and on they trudge.
So near! Yet nothing! Then how long? How
    long? ...

And slowly in his overheated mind
Peace like a river through the desert flows,
And sweetness wells and overflows in streams
That reach the farthest friend in memory.
Peace now, and dear delight in serving these,
These poor sheep, driven innocent to death:
Peace undisturbed, though the poor senses
    jump,
And horror catches at the heart as when
Death unsuspected flaunts his grisly hand
Under the very eye of quietness:
Peace, peace with all, even the enemy,
Compassion for them deep as for his own:
Quietness now amid the thunderous noise,
And sweet elation in the grave of gloom.

Jessie Pope

The Call

Who's for the trench –
 Are you, my laddie?
Who'll follow French –
 Will you, my laddie?
Who's fretting to begin,
Who's going out to win?
And who wants to save his skin –
 Do you, my laddie?

Who's for the khaki suit –
 Are you, my laddie?
Who longs to charge and shoot –
 Do you, my laddie?
Who's keen on getting fit,
Who means to show his grit,
And who'd rather wait a bit –
 Would you, my laddie?

Who'll earn the Empire's thanks –
 Will you, my laddie?
Who'll swell the victor's ranks –
 Will you, my laddie?
When that procession comes,
Banners and rolling drums –
Who'll stand and bite his thumbs –
 Will you, my laddie?

Edgell Rickword

The Soldier Addresses His Body

I shall be mad if you get smashed about,
we've had good times together, you and I;
although you groused a bit when luck was out,
say a girl turned us down, or we went dry.

But there's a world of things we haven't done,
countries not seen, where people do strange things;
eat fish alive, and mimic in the sun
the solemn gestures of their stone-grey kings.

I've heard of forests that are dim at noon
where snakes and creepers wrestle all day long;
where vivid beasts grow pale with the full moon,
gibber and cry, and wail a mad old song,

because at the full moon the Hippogriff
with wrinkled ivory snout and agate feet,
with his green eye will glare them cold and stiff
for the coward Wyvern to come down and eat.

Vodka, kvass or bitter mountain wines
we've never drunk; nor snatched the bursting grapes
to pelt slim girls among Sicilian vines,
who'd flicker through the leaves, faint frolic shapes.

Yes, there's a world of things we've never done,
but it's a sweat to knock them into rhyme,
let's have a drink, and give them cards a run
and leave dull verse to the dull peaceful time.

Edgell Rickword

Trench Poets

I knew a man, he was my chum,
But he grew blacker every day,
And would not brush the flies away,
Nor blanch however fierce the hum
Of passing shells; I used to read,
To rouse him, random things from Donne;
Like 'Get with child a mandrake-root,'
But you can tell he was far gone,
For he lay gaping, mackerel-eyed,
And stiff, and senseless as a post
Even when that old poet cried
'I long to talk with some old lover's ghost.'

I tried the Elegies one day,
But he, because he heard me say
'What needst thou have more covering than a man?'
Grinned nastily, and so I knew
The worms had got his brains at last.
There was one thing that I might do
To starve the worms; I racked my head
For healthy things and quoted *'Maud.'*
His grin got worse and I could see
He sneered at passion's purity.
He stank so badly, though we were great chums
I had to leave him; then rats ate his thumbs.

Edgell Rickword

War and Peace

In sodden trenches I have heard men speak,
Though numb and wretched, wise and witty things;
And loved them for the stubbornness that clings
Longest to laughter when Death's pulleys creak;

And seeing cool nurses move on tireless feet
To do abominable things with grace,
Deemed them sweet sisters in that haunted place
Where, with child's voices, strong men howl or bleat.

Yet now those men lay stubborn courage by,
Riding dull-eyed and silent in the train
To old men's stools; or sell gay-coloured socks
And listen fearfully for Death; so I
Love the low-laughing girls, who now again
Go daintily, in thin and flowery frocks.

Edgell Rickword

Winter Warfare

Colonel Cold strode up the Line
(Tabs of rime and spurs of ice),
Stiffened all where he did glare,
Horses, men, and lice.

Visited a forward post,
Left them burning, ear to foot;
Fingers stuck to biting steel,
Toes to frozen boot.

Stalked on into No Man's Land,
Turned the wire to fleecy wool,
Iron stakes to sugar sticks
Snapping at a pull.

Those who watched with hoary eyes
Saw two figures gleaming there;
Hauptman Kälte, Colonel Cold,
Gaunt, in the grey air.

Stiffly, tinkling spurs they moved
Glassy eyed, with glinting heel
Stabbing those who lingered there
Torn by screaming steel.

Isaac Rosenberg

Break of Day in the Trenches

The darkness crumbles away –
It is the same old druid Time as ever.
Only a live thing leaps my hand –
A queer sardonic rat –
As I pull the parapet's poppy
To stick behind my ear.
Droll rat, they would shoot you if they knew
Your cosmopolitan sympathies
(And God knows what antipathies).
Now you have touched this English hand
You will do the same to a German –
Soon, no doubt, if it be your pleasure
To cross the sleeping green between.
It seems you inwardly grin as you pass
Strong eyes, fine limbs, haughty athletes
Less chanced than you for life,
Bonds to the whims of murder,
Sprawled in the bowels of the earth,
The torn fields of France.
What do you see in our eyes
At the shrieking iron and flame
Hurled through still heavens?
What quaver – what heart aghast?
Poppies whose roots are in man's veins
Drop, and are ever dropping;
But mine in my ear is safe,
Just a little white with the dust.

Isaac Rosenberg

Dead Man's Dump

The plunging limbers over the shattered track
Racketed with their rusty freight,
Stuck out like many crowns of thorns,
And the rusty stakes like sceptres old
To stay the flood of brutish men
Upon our brothers dear.

The wheels lurched over sprawled dead
But pained them not, though their bones crunched,
Their shut mouths made no moan.
They lie there huddled, friend and foeman,
Man born of man, and born of woman,
And shells go crying over them
From night till night and now.

Earth has waited for them,
All the time of their growth
Fretting for their decay:
Now she has them at last!
In the strength of their strength
Suspended – stopped and held.

What fierce imaginings their dark souls lit?
Earth! have they gone into you!
Somewhere they must have gone,
And flung on your hard back
Is their soul's sack
Emptied of God-ancestralled essences.
Who hurled them out? Who hurled?

None saw their spirits' shadow shake the grass,
Or stood aside for the half used life to pass
Out of those doomed nostrils and the doomed
    mouth,
When the swift iron burning bee
Drained the wild honey of their youth.

What of us who, flung on the shrieking pyre,
Walk, our usual thoughts untouched,
Our lucky limbs as on ichor fed,
Immortal seeming ever?
Perhaps when the flames beat loud on us,
A fear may choke in our veins
And the startled blood may stop.

The air is loud with death,
The dark air spurts with fire,
The explosions ceaseless are.
Timelessly now, some minutes past,
Those dead strode time with vigorous life,
Till the shrapnel called 'An end!'
But not to all. In bleeding pangs
Some borne on stretchers dreamed of home,
Dear things, war-blotted from their hearts.

Maniac Earth! howling and flying, your bowel
Seared by the jagged fire, the iron love,
The impetuous storm of savage love.
Dark Earth! dark Heavens! swinging in chemic
    smoke,
What dead are born when you kiss each soundless
    soul
With lightning and thunder from your mined heart,
Which man's self dug, and his blind fingers loosed?

A man's brains splattered on
A stretcher-bearer's face;
His shook shoulders slipped their load,
But when they bent to look again
The drowning soul was sunk too deep
For human tenderness.

They left this dead with the older dead,
Stretched at the cross roads.

Burnt black by strange decay
Their sinister faces lie,
The lid over each eye,
The grass and coloured clay
More motion have than they,
Joined to the great sunk silences.

Here is one not long dead;
His dark hearing caught our far wheels,
And the choked soul stretched weak hands
To reach the living word the far wheels said,
The blood-dazed intelligence beating for light,
Crying through the suspense of the far torturing
    wheels
Swift for the end to break
Or the wheels to break,
Cried as the tide of the world broke over his sight.

Will they come? Will they ever come?
Even as the mixed hoofs of the mules,
The quivering-bellied mules,
And the rushing wheels all mixed
With his tortured upturned sight.
So we crashed round the bend,
We heard his weak scream,
We heard his very last sound,
And our wheels grazed his dead face.

Isaac Rosenberg

In the Trenches

I snatched two poppies
From the parapet's edge,
Two bright red poppies
That winked on the ledge.

Behind my ear
I stuck one through,
One blood red poppy
I gave to you.

The sandbags narrowed
And screwed out our jest,
And tore the poppy
You had on your breast …
Dawn – a shell – O! Christ
I am choked … safe … dust blind, I
See trench floor poppies
Strewn. Smashed, you lie.

Isaac Rosenberg

Louse Hunting

Nudes – stark and glistening,
Yelling in lurid glee. Grinning faces
And raging limbs
Whirl over the floor one fire.
For a shirt verminously busy
Yon soldier tore from his throat, with oaths
Godhead might shrink at, but not the lice.
And soon the shirt was aflare
Over the candle he'd lit while we lay.

Then we all sprang up and stript
To hunt the verminous brood.
Soon like a demons' pantomime
The place was raging.
See the silhouettes agape,
See the gibbering shadows
Mixed with the battled arms on the wall.
See gargantuan hooked fingers
Pluck in supreme flesh
To smutch supreme littleness.
See the merry limbs in hot Highland fling
Because some wizard vermin
Charmed from the quiet this revel
When our ears were half lulled
By the dark music
Blown from Sleep's trumpet.

Isaac Rosenberg

Returning, We Hear the Larks

Sombre the night is.
And though we have our lives, we know
What sinister threat lies there.

Dragging these anguished limbs, we only know
This poison-blasted track opens on our camp –
On a little safe sleep.

But hark! joy – joy – strange joy.
Lo! heights of night ringing with unseen larks.
Music showering our upturned list'ning faces.

Death could drop from the dark
As easily as song –
But song only dropped,
Like a blind man's dreams on the sand
By dangerous tides,
Like a girl's dark hair for she dreams no ruin lies
        there,
Or her kisses where a serpent hides.

Isaac Rosenberg

The Immortals

I killed them, but they would not die.
Yea! all the day and all the night
For them I could not rest or sleep,
Nor guard from them nor hide in flight.

Then in my agony I turned
And made my hands red in their gore.
In vain – for faster than I slew
They rose more cruel than before.

I killed and killed with slaughter mad;
I killed till all my strength was gone.
And still they rose to torture me,
For Devils only die in fun.

I used to think the Devil hid
In women's smiles and wine's carouse.
I called him Satan, Balzebub.
But now I call him, dirty louse.

Gerald Samuel

Life and Death

Life and Death were playing,
　And Life had seemed to win,
Until, her progress staying,
Death mocked her tears and praying,
And gaily went on slaying,
　With triumph in his grin.

Yet Life still went on gaining,
　And Death seemed in despair,
Until, no longer feigning
To feel his luck was waning,
A loathsome plague unchaining,
　He poisoned all the air.

But Life was not defeated,
　And ceaseless efforts made.
But Death would not be cheated,
And all his wiles repeated,
And made men's passions heated,
　Till War gave him its aid.

And so through all the ages
　Shall Life and Death contend,
And while the battle rages,
In vain we turn the pages,
For not the wisest sages
　Shall ever learn the end.

Siegfried Sassoon

Aftermath

Have you forgotten yet? ...
For the world's events have rumbled on since those
    gagged days,
Like traffic checked while at the crossing of city-
    ways:
And the haunted gap in your mind has filled with
    thoughts that flow
Like clouds in the lit heaven of life; and you're a man
    reprieved to go,
Taking your peaceful share of Time, with joy to
    spare.
*But the past is just the same – and War's a bloody
    game ...*
Have you forgotten yet? ...
*Look down, and swear by the slain of the War that you'll
    never forget.*

Do you remember the dark months you held the
    sector at Mametz –
The nights you watched and wired and dug and
    piled sandbags on parapets?
Do you remember the rats; and the stench
Of corpses rotting in front of the front-line trench –
And dawn coming, dirty-white, and chill with a
    hopeless rain?
Do you ever stop and ask, 'Is it all going to happen
    again?'

Do you remember that hour of din before the
    attack –
And the anger, the blind compassion that seized and
    shook you then
As you peered at the doomed and haggard faces of
    your men?
Do you remember the stretcher-cases lurching back
With dying eyes and lolling heads – those ashen-
    grey
Masks of the lads who once were keen and kind and
    gay?

Have you forgotten yet? …
Look up, and swear by the green of the spring that you'll
    never forget.

Siegfried Sassoon

Attack

At dawn the ridge emerges massed and dun
In the wild purple of the glow'ring sun,
Smouldering through spouts of drifting smoke that
    shroud
The menacing scarred slope; and, one by one,
Tanks creep and topple forward to the wire.
The barrage roars and lifts. Then, clumsily bowed
With bombs and guns and shovels and battle-gear,
Men jostle and climb to meet the bristling fire.
Lines of grey, muttering faces, masked with fear,
They leave their trenches, going over the top,
While time ticks blank and busy on their wrists,
And hope, with furtive eyes and grappling fists,
Flounders in mud. O Jesus, make it stop!

Siegfried Sassoon

Base Details

If I were fierce, and bald, and short of breath,
  I'd live with scarlet Majors at the Base,
And speed glum heroes up the line to death.
  You'd see me with my puffy petulant face,
Guzzling and gulping in the best hotel,
  Reading the Roll of Honour. 'Poor young chap,'
I'd say – 'I used to know his father well;
  Yes, we've lost heavily in this last scrap.'
And when the war is done and youth stone dead,
I'd toddle safely home and die – in bed.

Siegfried Sassoon

Counter-Attack

We'd gained our first objective hours before
While dawn broke like a face with blinking eyes,
Pallid, unshaved and thirsty, blind with smoke.
Things seemed all right at first. We held their line,
With bombers posted, Lewis guns well placed,
And clink of shovels deepening the shallow trench.
    The place was rotten with dead; green clumsy legs
      High-booted, sprawled and grovelled along the
        saps
    And trunks, face downward, in the sucking mud,
    Wallowed like trodden sand-bags loosely filled;
    And naked sodden buttocks, mats of hair,
    Bulged, clotted heads slept in the plastering slime,
    And then the rain began, – the jolly old rain!

A yawning soldier knelt against the bank,
Staring across the morning blear with fog;
He wondered when the Allemands would get busy;
And then, of course, they started with five-nines
Traversing, sure as fate, and never a dud.
Mute in the clamour of shells he watched them burst
Spouting dark earth and wire with gusts from hell,
While posturing giants dissolved in drifts of smoke.
He crouched and flinched, dizzy with galloping fear,
Sick for escape, – loathing the strangled horror
And butchered, frantic gestures of the dead.

An officer came blundering down the trench:
'Stand-to and man the fire-step!' On he went …
Gasping and bawling, 'Fire-step … counter-attack!'

    Then the haze lifted. Bombing on the right
    Down the old sap: machine-guns on the left;
    And stumbling figures looming out in front.
    'O Christ, they're coming at us!' Bullets spat,
And he remembered his rifle … rapid fire …
And started blazing wildly … then a bang
Crumpled and spun him sideways, knocked him out
To grunt and wriggle: none heeded him; he choked
And fought the flapping veils of smothering gloom,
Lost in a blurred confusion of yells and groans …
Down, and down, and down, he sank and drowned,
Bleeding to death. The counter-attack had failed.

Siegfried Sassoon

Died of Wounds

His wet white face and miserable eyes
Brought nurses to him more than groans and sighs:
But hoarse and low and rapid rose and fell
His troubled voice: he did the business well.

The ward grew dark; but he was still complaining
And calling out for 'Dickie'. 'Curse the Wood!
It's time to go. O Christ, and what's the good?
We'll never take it, and it's always raining.'

I wondered where he'd been; then heard him shout,
'They snipe like hell! O Dickie, don't go out' …
I fell asleep … Next morning he was dead;
And some Slight Wound lay smiling on the bed.

Siegfried Sassoon

Does it Matter?

Does it matter? – losing your legs? …
For people will always be kind,
And you need not show that you mind
When the others come in after football
To gobble their muffins and eggs.

Does it matter? – losing your sight? …
There's such splendid work for the blind;
And people will always be kind,
As you sit on the terrace remembering
And turning your face to the light.

Do they matter? – those dreams from the pit? …
You can drink and forget and be glad,
And people won't say that you're mad;
For they'll know you've fought for your country
And no one will worry a bit.

Siegfried Sassoon

Glory of Women

You love us when we're heroes, home on leave,
Or wounded in a mentionable place.
You worship decorations; you believe
That chivalry redeems the war's disgrace.
You make us shells. You listen with delight,
By tales of dirt and danger fondly thrilled.
You crown our distant ardours while we fight,
And mourn our laurelled memories when we're
    killed.
You can't believe that British troops 'retire'
When hell's last horror breaks them, and they run,
Trampling the terrible corpses – blind with blood.
  O German mother dreaming by the fire,
  While you are knitting socks to send your son
  His face is trodden deeper in the mud.

Siegfried Sassoon

On Passing the New Menin Gate

Who will remember, passing through this Gate,
The unheroic Dead who fed the guns?
Who shall absolve the foulness of their fate, –
Those doomed, conscripted, unvictorious ones?
   Crudely renewed, the Salient holds its own.
   Paid are its dim defenders by this pomp;
   Paid, with a pile of peace-complacent stone,
   The armies who endured that sullen swamp.

Here was the world's worst wound. And here with
     pride
'Their name liveth for ever,' the Gateway claims.
Was ever an immolation so belied
As these intolerably nameless names?
Well might the Dead who struggled in the slime
Rise and deride this sepulchre of crime.

Siegfried Sassoon

The General

'Good-morning; good-morning!' the General said
When we met him last week on our way to the line.
Now the soldiers he smiled at are most of 'em dead,
And we're cursing his staff for incompetent swine.
'He's a cheery old card,' grunted Harry to Jack
As they slogged up to Arras with rifle and pack.

But he did for them both by his plan of attack.

Siegfried Sassoon

The Hero

'Jack fell as he'd have wished,' the Mother said,
And folded up the letter that she'd read.
'The Colonel writes so nicely.' Something broke
In the tired voice that quavered to a choke.
She half looked up. 'We mothers are so proud
Of our dead soldiers.' Then her face was bowed.

Quietly the Brother Officer went out.
He'd told the poor old dear some gallant lies
That she would nourish all her days, no doubt.
For while he coughed and mumbled, her weak eyes
Had shone with gentle triumph, brimmed with joy,
Because he'd been so brave, her glorious boy.

He thought how 'Jack', cold-footed, useless swine,
Had panicked down the trench that night the mine
Went up at Wicked Corner; how he'd tried
To get sent home, and how, at last, he died,
Blown to small bits. And no one seemed to care
Except that lonely woman with white hair.

Siegfried Sassoon

They

The Bishop tells us: 'When the boys come back
They will not be the same; for they'll have fought
In a just cause: they lead the last attack
On Anti-Christ; their comrades' blood has bought
New right to breed an honourable race.
They have challenged Death and dared him face to
    face.'

'We're none of us the same!' the boys reply.
'For George lost both his legs; and Bill's stone blind;
Poor Jim's shot through the lungs and like to die;
And Bert's gone syphilitic: you'll not find
A chap who's served that hasn't found *some* change.'
And the Bishop said: 'The ways of God are strange!'

Siegfried Sassoon

To Any Dead Officer

Well, how are things in Heaven? I wish you'd say,
Because I'd like to know that you're all right.
Tell me, have you found everlasting day,
Or been sucked in by everlasting night?
For when I shut my eyes your face shows pain;
I hear you make some cheery old remark –
I can rebuild you in my brain,
Though you've gone out patrolling in the dark.

You hated tours of trenches; you were proud
Of nothing more than having good years to spend;
Longed to get home and join the careless crowd
Of chaps who work in peace with Time for friend.
That's all washed out now. You're beyond the wire:
No earthly chance can send you crawling back;
You've finished with machine-gun fire –
Knocked over in a hopeless dud-attack.

Somehow I always thought you'd get done in,
Because you were so desperate keen to live:
You were all out to try and save your skin,
Well knowing how much the world had got to give.
You joked at shells and talked the usual 'shop,'
Stuck to your dirty job and did it fine:
With 'Jesus Christ! when_will_it stop?
Three years … It's hell unless we break their line.'

So when they told me you'd been left for dead
I wouldn't believe them, feeling it_must_be true.
Next week the bloody Roll of Honour said
'Wounded and missing' – (That's the thing to do
When lads are left in shell-holes dying slow,
With nothing but blank sky and wounds that ache,
Moaning for water till they know
It's night, and then it's not worth while to wake!)

*   *   *

Good-bye, old lad! Remember me to God,
And tell Him that our Politicians swear
They won't give in till Prussian Rule's been trod
Under the Heel of England … Are you there? …
Yes … and the War won't end for at least two years;
But we've got stacks of men … I'm blind with tears,
Staring into the dark. Cheero!
I wish they'd killed you in a decent show.

Siegfried Sassoon

To One Who Was With Me in the War

It was too long ago – that Company which we
     served with …
We call it back in visual fragments, you and I,
Who seem, ourselves, like relics casually preserved
     with
Our mindfulness of old bombardments when the sky
With blundering din blinked cavernous.

                      Yet sense of power
Invades us when, recapturing an ungodly hour
Of ante-zero crisis, in one thought we've met
To stand in some redoubt of Time, – to share again
All but the actual wetness of the flare-lit rain,
All but the living presences who haunt us yet
With gloom-patrolling eyes.

                    Remembering, we forget
Much that was monstrous, much that clogged our
     souls with clay
When hours were guides who led us by the longest
     way –
And when the worst had been endured could still
     disclose
Another worst to thwart us …

We forget our fear …

And, while the undercouth event begins to lour less
near,

Discern the mad magnificence whose storm-light
throws

Wild shadows on these after-thoughts that send
your brain

Back beyond peace, exploring sunken ruinous roads.

Your brain, with files of flitting forms hump-backed
with loads,

On its own helmet hears the tinkling drops of rain, –

Follows to an end some night relief, and strangely
sees

The quiet no-man's-land of daybreak, jagg'd with trees

That loom like giant Germans …

I'll go with you, then,

Since you must play this game of ghosts. At
listening-posts

We'll peer across dim craters; joke with jaded men

Whose names we've long forgotten. (Stoop low
there; it's the place

The sniper enfilades.) Round the next bay you'll meet

A drenched platoon-commander; chilled he drums
his feet

On squelching duck-boards; winds his wrist-watch;
turns his head,

And shows you how you looked, – your ten-years-
vanished face,

Hoping the War will end next week …

What's that you said?

Siegfried Sassoon

Trench Duty

Shaken from sleep, and numbed and scarce awake,
Out in the trench with three hours' watch to take,
I blunder through the splashing mirk; and then
Hear the gruff muttering voices of the men
Crouching in cabins candle-chinked with light.
Hark! There's the big bombardment on our right
Rumbling and bumping; and the dark's a glare
Of flickering horror in the sectors where
We raid the Boche; men waiting, stiff and chilled,
Or crawling on their bellies through the wire.
'What? Stretcher-bearers wanted? Someone killed?'
Five minutes ago I heard a sniper fire:
Why did he do it? ... Starlight overhead –
Blank stars. I'm wide-awake; and some chap's dead.

Siegfried Sassoon

Wirers

'Pass it along, the wiring party's going out' –
And yawning sentries mumble, 'Wirers going out,'
Unravelling; twisting; hammering stakes with
    muffled thud,
They toil with stealthy haste and anger in their
    blood.

The Boche sends up a flare. Black forms stand rigid
    there,
Stock-still like posts; then darkness, and the clumsy
    ghosts
Stride hither and thither, whispering, tripped by
    clutching snare
Of snags and tangles.
Ghastly dawn with vaporous coasts
Gleams desolate along the sky, night's misery ended.

Young Hughes was badly hit; I heard him carried
    away,
Moaning at every lurch; no doubt he'll die to-day.
But we can say the front-line wire's been safely
    mended.

Alan Seeger

Rendezvous

I have a rendezvous with Death
At some disputed barricade,
When Spring comes back with rustling shade
And apple-blossoms fill the air –
I have a rendezvous with Death
When Spring brings back blue days and fair.

It may be he shall take my hand
And lead me into his dark land
And close my eyes and quench my breath –
It may be I shall pass him still.
I have a rendezvous with Death
On some scarred slope of battered hill,
When Spring comes round again this year
And the first meadow-flowers appear.

God knows 'twere better to be deep
Pillowed in silk and scented down,
Where love throbs out in blissful sleep,
Pulse nigh to pulse, and breath to breath,
Where hushed awakenings are dear …
But I've a rendezvous with Death
At midnight in some flaming town,
When Spring trips north again this year,
And I to my pledged word am true,
I shall not fail that rendezvous.

Alan Seeger

On Returning to the Front After Leave

Apart sweet women (for whom Heaven be blessed),
Comrades, you cannot think how thin and blue
Look the leftovers of mankind that rest,
Now that the cream has been skimmed off in you.
War has its horrors, but has this of good –
That its sure processes sort out and bind
Brave hearts in one intrepid brotherhood
And leave the shams and imbeciles behind.
Now turn we joyful to the great attacks,
Not only that we face in a fair field
Our valiant foe and all his deadly tools,
But also that we turn disdainful backs
On that poor world we scorn yet die to shield –
That world of cowards, hypocrites, and fools.

Patrick Shaw-Stewart

I Saw a Man

I saw a man this morning
    Who did not wish to die:
I ask, and cannot answer,
    If otherwise wish I.

Fair broke the day this morning
    Against the Dardanelles;
The breeze blew soft, the morn's cheeks
    Were cold as cold sea-shells.

But other shells are waiting
    Across the Aegean Sea,
Shrapnel and high explosive,
    Shells and hells for me.

O hell of ships and cities,
    Hell of men like me,
Fatal second Helen,
    Why must I follow thee?

Achilles came to Troyland
    And I to Chersonese:
He turned from wrath to battle,
    And I from three days' peace.

Was it so hard, Achilles,
   So very hard to die?
Thou knowest and I know not –
   So much the happier am I.

I will go back this morning
   From Imbros over the sea;
Stand in the trench, Achilles,
   Flame-capped, and shout for me.

Gallipoli; killed in action, 1917

Osbert Sitwell

Arm-chair

If I were now of handsome middle-age,
I should not govern yet, but still should hope
To help the prosecution of this war.
I'd talk and eat (though not eat wheaten bread),
I'd send my sons, if old enough, to France,
Or help to do my share in other ways.
All through the long spring evenings, when the sun
Pursued its primrose path toward the hills,
If fine, I'd plant potatoes on the lawn;
If wet, write anxious letters to the Press.
I'd give up wine and spirits, and with pride
Refuse to eat meat more than once a day,
And seek to rob the workers of their beer.
The only way to win a hard-fought war
Is to annoy the people in small ways,
Bully or patronize them, as you will!
I'd teach poor mothers, who have seven sons
– All fighting men of clean and sober life –
How to look after babies and to cook;
Teach them to save their money and invest;
Not to bring children up in luxury
– But do without a nursemaid in the house!

If I were old or only seventy,
Then should I be a great man in his prime.
I should rule army corps; at my command
Men would rise up, salute me, and attack
– And die. Or I might also govern men
By making speeches with my toothless jaws,
Constant in chatter, until men should say,
'One grand old man is still worth half his pay!'
That day, I'd send my grandsons out to France
– And wish I'd got ten other ones to send
(One cannot sacrifice too much, I'd say).
Then would I make a noble, toothless speech,
And all the list'ning Parliament would cheer.
'We cannot and we will not end this war
Till all the younger men with martial mien
Have enter'd capitals; never make peace
Till they are cripples, on one leg, or dead!'
Then would the Bishops go nigh mad with joy,
Cantuar, Ebor, and the other ones,
Be overwhelmed with pious ecstasy
In thanking Him we'd got a Christian,
An Englishman, still worth his salt, to talk.
In every pulpit would they preach and prance;
And our great Church would work, as heretofore,
To bring this poor old nation to its knees.
Then we'd forbid all liberty, and make
Free speech a relic of our impious past;
And when this war is finished, when the world
Is torn and bleeding, cut and bruised to death,
Then I'd pronounce my peace terms – to the poor!

But as it is, I am not ninety yet,
And so must pay my reverence to these men –
These grand old men, who still can see and talk,
Who sacrifice each other's sons each day.
O Lord! let me be ninety yet, I pray.
Methuselah was quite a youngster when
He died. Now, vainly weeping, we should say:
'Another great man perished in his prime!'
O let me govern, Lord, at ninety-nine!

Hugh Smith

The Incorrigibles

(Written from the Front to a Friend)

Keen through the shell-hole in my billet walls
The sad, dirge-laden wind of Flanders calls
(Hark! Ere the words are written, have replied
The rumblings of my supperless inside!)
Keen (as I think I said) the north wind bellows,
And makes me envy all you lucky fellows
Who quaff at ease your bitters and your gin
Before you put your grill-room dinners in.
Spake one to me and prated how that all
In war was Glory, Triumph and Trumpet-call;
And said that Death, who stalked across the field,
But sowed, that Life a nobler crop might yield!
Poor Vapourer! for now I know that he
Was on the Staff or in the A.S.C.,
And in a well-manured hot-bed grew –
The ginger-bread is gilded but for few!
For us, foot-slogging sadly, it is clear
That War is fleas, short rations, watered beer,
Noise and mismanagement, bluster and foreboding,
Triumph but the sequel to enough exploding.
Yet like a ray across a storm-torn sea
Shines through it all the glint of Comedy,
And pompous Death, whose table they have
      messed at,
Has given the Men another butt to jest at!

Charles Sorley

All the Hills and Vales Along

All the hills and vales along
Earth is bursting into song,
And the singers are the chaps
Who are going to die perhaps.
    O sing, marching men,
    Till the valleys ring again.
    Give your gladness to earth's keeping,
    So be glad, when you are sleeping.

Cast away regret and rue,
Think what you are marching to,
Little give, great pass.
Jesus Christ and Barabbas
Were found the same day.
This died, that, went his way.
    So sing with joyful breath.
    For why, you are going to death.
    Teeming earth will surely store
    All the gladness that you pour.

Earth that never doubts nor fears
Earth that knows of death, not tears,
Earth that bore with joyful ease
Hemlock for Socrates,
Earth that blossomed and was glad
'Neath the cross that Christ had,
Shall rejoice and blossom too
When the bullet reaches you.
    Wherefore, men marching
    On the road to death, sing!
    Pour gladness on earth's head,
    So be merry, so be dead.

From the hills and valleys earth
Shouts back the sound of mirth,
Tramp of feet and lilt of song
Ringing all the road along.
All the music of their going,
Ringing swinging glad song-throwing,
Earth will echo still, when foot
Lies numb and voice mute.
    On marching men, on
    To the gates of death with song.
    Sow your gladness for earth's reaping,
    So you may be glad though sleeping.
    Strew your gladness on earth's bed,
    So be merry, so be dead.

Charles Sorley

In Memoriam S.C.W., V.C.

(8 September 1915)

There is no fitter end than this.
   No need is now to yearn nor sigh.
We know the glory that is his,
   A glory that can never die.

Surely we knew it long before,
   Knew all along that he was made
For a swift radiant morning, for
   A sacrificing swift night-shade.

Charles Sorley

Such, Such is Death

Such, such is Death: no triumph: no defeat:
Only an empty pail, a slate rubbed clean,
A merciful putting away of what has been.

And this we know: Death is not Life effete,
Life crushed, the broken pail. We who have seen
So marvellous things know well the end not yet.

Victor and vanquished are a-one in death:
Coward and brave: friend, foe. Ghosts do not say
'Come, what was your record when you drew breath?'
But a big blot has hid each yesterday
So poor, so manifestly incomplete.
And your bright Promise, withered long and sped,
Is touched, stirs, rises, opens and grows sweet
And blossoms and is you, when you are dead.

Charles Sorley

Light-Lipped and Singing

Light-lipped and singing press we hard
Over old earth which now is worn,
Triumphant, buffetted and scarred,
By billows howled at, tempest-torn,
Toward blue horizons far away
(Which do not give the rest we need,
But some long strife, more than this play,
Some task that will be stern indeed) –
We ever new, we ever young,
We happy creatures of a day!
What will the gods say, seeing us strung
As nobly and as taut as they?

Charles Sorley

To Germany

You are blind like us. Your hurt no man designed,
And no man claimed the conquest of your land.
But gropers both through fields of thought confined
We stumble and we do not understand.
You only saw your future bigly planned,
And we, the tapering paths of our own mind,
And in each other's dearest ways we stand,
And hiss and hate. And the blind fight the blind.

When it is peace, then we may view again
With new-won eyes each other's truer form
And wonder. Grown more loving-kind and warm
We'll grasp firm hands and laugh at the old pain,
When it is peace. But until peace, the storm
The darkness and the thunder and the rain.

Charles Sorley

When You See millions of the Mouthless Dead

When you see millions of the mouthless dead
Across your dreams in pale battalions go,
Say not soft things as other men have said,
That you'll remember. For you need not so.
Give them not praise. For, deaf, how should they
    know
It is not curses heaped on each gashed head?
Nor tears. Their blind eyes see not your tears flow.
Nor honour. It is easy to be dead.
Say only this, 'They are dead.' Then add thereto,
'yet many a better one has died before.'
Then, scanning all the overcrowded mass, should you
Perceive one face that you loved heretofore,
It is a spook. None wears the face you knew.
Great death has made all this for evermore.

J.C. Squire

The Dilemma

God heard the embattled nations sing and shout
'Gott strafe England!' and 'God save the King!'
God this, God that, and God the other thing –
'Good God!' said God 'I've got my work cut out.'

J.E. Stewart

On Revisiting the Somme

If I were but a Journalist,
And had a heading every day
In double-column caps, I wist
I, too, could make it pay;

But still for me the shadow lies
Of tragedy. I cannot write
Of these so many Calvaries
As of a pageant fight;

For dead men look me through and through
With their blind eyes, and mutely cry
My name, as I were one they knew
In that red-rimmed July;

Others on new sensation bent
Will wander here, with some glib guide
Insufferably eloquent
Of secrets we would hide –

Hide in this battered crumbling line
Hide in these promiscuous graves,
Till one shall make our story shine
In the fierce light it craves.

E. Wyndham Tennant

The Mad Soldier

I dropp'd here three weeks ago, yes – I know,
And it's bitter cold at night, since the fight –
I could tell you if I chose – no one knows
Excep' me and four or five, what ain't alive
I can see them all asleep, three men deep,
And they're nowhere near a fire – but our wire
Has 'em fast as fast can be. Can't you see
When the flare goes up? Ssh! Boys; what's that
    noise?
Do you know what these rats eat? Body-meat!
After you've been down a week, 'an your cheek
Gets as pale as life, and night seems as white
As the day, only the rats and their brats
Seem more hungry when the day's gone away –
An' they look as big as bulls, an' they pulls
Till you almost sort o' shout – but the drought
What you hadn't felt before makes you sore.

And at times you even think of a drink ...
There's a leg acrost my thighs – if my eyes
Weren't too sore, I'd like to see who it be,
Wonder if I'd know the bloke if I woke? –
Woke? By damn, I'm not asleep – there's a heap
Of us wond'ring why the hell we're not well ...
Leastways I am – since I came it's the same
With the others – they don't know what I do,
Or they wouldn't gape and grin. – It's a sin
To say that Hell is hot – 'cause it's not:
Mind you, I know very well we're in hell.
– In a twisted hump we lie – heaping high
Yes! an' higher every day. – Oh, I say,
This chap's heavy on my thighs – damn his eyes.

Edward Thomas

A Private

This ploughman dead in battle slept out of doors
Many a frozen night, and merrily
Answered staid drinkers, good bedmen, and all
     bores:
'At Mrs Greenland's Hawthorn Bush,' said he,
'I slept.' None knew which bush. Above the town,
Beyond 'The Drover,' a hundred spot the down
In Wiltshire. And where now at last he sleeps
More sound in France – that, too, he secret keeps.

Edward Thomas

As the Team's Head-Brass

As the team's head-brass flashed out on the turn
The lovers disappeared into the wood.
I sat among the boughs of the fallen elm
That strewed an angle of the fallow, and
Watched the plough narrowing a yellow square
Of charlock. Every time the horses turned
Instead of treading me down, the ploughman leaned
Upon the handles to say or ask a word,
About the weather, next about the war.
Scraping the share he faced towards the wood,
And screwed along the furrow till the brass flashed
Once more.
        The blizzard felled the elm whose crest
I sat in, by a woodpecker's round hole,
The ploughman said. 'When will they take it away?'
'When the war's over.' So the talk began –
One minute and an interval of ten,
A minute more and the same interval.
'Have you been out?' 'No.' 'And don't want to,
    perhaps?'
'If I could only come back again, I should.
I could spare an arm. I shouldn't want to lose
A leg. If I should lose my head, why, so,
I should want nothing more … Have many gone
From here?' 'Yes.' 'Many lost?' 'Yes: good few.
Only two teams work on the farm this year.

One of my mates is dead. The second day
In France they killed him. It was back in March,
The very night of the blizzard, too. Now if
He had stayed here we should have moved the tree.'
'And I should not have sat here. Everything
Would have been different. For it would have been
Another world.' 'Ay, and a better, though
If we could see all all might seem good.' Then
The lovers came out of the wood again:
The horses started and for the last time
I watched the clods crumble and topple over
After the ploughshare and the stumbling team.

Edward Thomas

In Memoriam

The flowers left thick at nightfall in the wood
This Eastertide call into mind the men,
Now far from home, who, with their sweethearts, should
     should
Have gathered them and will do never again.

Edward Thomas

Lights Out

I have come to the borders of sleep,
The unfathomable deep
Forest where all must lose
Their way, however straight,
Or winding, soon or late;
They cannot choose.

Many a road and track
That, since the dawn's first crack,
Up to the forest brink,
Deceived the travellers,
Suddenly now blurs,
And in they sink.

Here love ends,
Despair, ambition ends,
All pleasure and all trouble,
Although most sweet or bitter,
Here ends in sleep that is sweeter
Than tasks most noble.

There is not any book
Or face of dearest look
That I would not turn from now
To go into the unknown
I must enter and leave alone
I know not how.

The tall forest towers;
Its cloudy foliage lowers
Ahead, shelf above shelf;
Its silence I hear and obey
That I may lose my way
And myself.

Edward Thomas

No One Cares Less Than I

'No one cares less than I,
Nobody knows but God,
Whether I am destined to lie
Under a foreign clod,'
Were the words I made to the bugle call in the
      morning.

But laughing, storming, scorning,
Only the bugles know
What the bugles say in the morning,
And they do not care, when they blow
The call that I heard and made words to early this
      morning.

Edward Thomas

The Cherry Trees

The cherry trees bend over and are shedding,
On the old road where all that passed are dead,
Their petals, strewing the grass as for a wedding
This early May morn when there is none to wed.

Edward Thomas

The Owl

Downhill I came, hungry, and yet not starved;
Cold, yet had heat within me that was proof
Against the North wind; tired, yet so that rest
Had seemed the sweetest thing under a roof.

Then at the inn I had food, fire, and rest,
Knowing how hungry, cold, and tired was I.
All of the night was quite barred out except
An owl's cry, a most melancholy cry

Shaken out long and clear upon the hill,
No merry note, nor cause of merriment,
But one telling me plain what I escaped
And others could not, that night, as in I went.

And salted was my food, and my repose,
Salted and sobered, too, by the bird's voice
Speaking for all who lay under the stars,
Soldiers and poor, unable to rejoice.

Edward Thomas

This is No Case of Petty Right or Wrong

This is no case of petty right or wrong
That politicians or philosophers
Can judge. I hate not Germans, nor grow hot
With love of Englishmen, to please newspapers.
Beside my hate for one fat patriot
My hatred of the Kaiser is love true:–
A kind of god he is, banging a gong.
But I have not to choose between the two,
Or between justice and injustice. Dinned
With war and argument I read no more
Than in the storm smoking along the wind
Athwart the wood. Two witches' cauldrons roar.
From one the weather shall rise clear and gay;
Out of the other an England beautiful
And like her mother that died yesterday.

Little I know or care if, being dull,
I shall miss something that historians
Can rake out of the ashes when perchance
The phoenix broods serene above their ken.
But with the best and meanest Englishmen
I am one in crying, God save England, lest
We lose what never slaves and cattle blessed.
The ages made her that made us from dust:
She is all we know and live by, and we trust
She is good and must endure, loving her so:
And as we love ourselves we hate our foe.

Robert Vernède

At Delville

At Delville I lost three Sergeants –
And never within my ken
Had one of them taken thought for his life
Or cover for aught but his men.

Not for two years of fighting
Through that devilish strain and noise;
Yet one of them called out as he died –
'I've been so ambitious, boys' ...

And I thought to myself, 'Ambitious!'
Did he mean that he longed for power?
But I knew that he'd never thought of himself
Save in his dying hour.

And one left a note for his mother,
Saying he gladly died
For England, and wished no better thing ...
How she must weep with pride.

And one with never a word fell,
Talking's the one thing he'd shirk,
But I never knew him other than keen
For things like danger and work.

Those Sergeants I lost at Delville
On a night that was cruel and black,
They gave their lives for England's sake,
They will never come back.

What of the hundreds in whose hearts
Thoughts no less splendid burn? …
I wonder what England will do for them
If ever they return?

Robert Vernède

A Listening Post

The sun's a red ball in the oak
   And all the grass is grey with dew,
Awhile ago a blackbird spoke –
   He didn't know the world's askew.

And yonder rifleman and I
   Wait here behind the misty trees
To shoot the first man that goes by,
   Our rifles ready on our knees.

How could he know that if we fail
   The world may lie in chains for years
And England be a bygone tale
   And right be wrong, and laughter tears?

Strange that this bird sits there and sings
   While we must only sit and plan –
Who are so much the higher things –
   The murder of our fellow man …

But maybe God will cause to be –
   Who brought forth sweetness from the strong –
Out of our discords harmony
   Sweeter than that bird's song.

Gilbert Waterhouse

Rail-Head

Someville is the Rail-head for bully beef and tea,
Matches and candles, and (good for you and me)
Cocoa and coffee and biscuits by the tin,
Sardines, condensed milk, petrol and paraffin.
Truck-load and train-load and lorries by the score,
Mule-cart and limber, 'What are yer waitin' for?'
Dusty and dirty and full of noisy din,
'If 'e fights upon 'is stomach, this 'ere army oughter
    win!'
Someville is the Rail-head, full of noisy din,
Full of men and horses and mules and paraffin,
Frozen meat and apricots and peaches-a-la-tin,
Shunting up and down, across, and round and out
    and in.
But down beyond the Rail-head and village of that
    name,
Are green woods, where the cuckoo is calling just the
    same,
As he used to call in April, in the years before the
    war,
And he calls the same as ever now and doesn't care
    a straw,
Down the green and leafy lanes, where Jean and his
    Marcelle
In Spring-time would wander, their loving vows to
    tell.

But petite Marcelle now is up, and working on the
    farm,
With only the memory of Jean's encircling arm,
Only comfort, chilling comfort, can little Marcelle
    draw,
And cuckoos are calling, and never care a straw;
And Tommy says that girl Marcelle, indeed she is
    'no bonn,'
Because Marcelle 'no promenade' with any mother's
    son;
Because petite Marcelle, he says, is always cross and
    sad,
When cuckoos are calling and all the woods are glad.
And madame, the mother of dark-eyed, sad
    Marcelle,
She ain't what yer'd call now a petite demoiselle,
'Gor blimy, she ain't, no!' says Tommy. 'She's narpoo!
A-scoldin' 'er daughter, an' makin' such terdoo!'
But mother and daughter, tho' Tommy doesn't see,
Are held by the bond of a common memory,
A husband, a father, a lover, and a son.
The war barely started, and all were up and gone,
And mother and daughter now work upon the farms,
With only the memory of those encircling arms.

Someville is the Rail-head for tea and bully beef,
Dusty and dirty, with all the woods in leaf
In April, sweet April, and all the world at war,
And cuckoos a-calling and never care a straw.

Arthur Graeme West

God, How I Hate You

God! how I hate you, you young cheerful men,
Whose pious poetry blossoms on your graves
As soon as you are in them …
                              Hark how one chants –
'Oh happy to have lived these epic days' –
'These epic days'! And *he'd* been to France,
And seen the trenches, glimpsed the huddled dead
In the periscope, hung on the rusty wire:
Choked by their sickly foetor, day and night
Blown down his throat: stumbled through ruined
    hearths,
Proved all that muddy brown monotony
Where blood's the only coloured thing. Perhaps
Had seen a man killed, a sentry shot at night,
Hunched as he fell, his feet on the firing-step,
His neck against the back slope of the trench,
And the rest doubled between, his head
Smashed like an eggshell! and the warm grey brain
Spattered all bloody on the parados …
Yet still God's in His Heaven, all is right
In this best possible of worlds …
God loves us, God looks down on this our strife
And smiles in pity, blows a pipe at times
And calls some warriors home …

How rare life is!
On earth, the love and fellowship of men,
Men sternly banded: banded for what end?
Banded to maim and kill their fellow men –
For even Huns are men. In Heaven above
A genial umpire, a good judge of sport
Won't let us hurt each other! Let's rejoice
God keeps us faithful, pens us still in fold.
Ah, what a faith is ours (almost, it seems,
Large as a mustard seed) – we trust and trust,
Nothing can shake us! Ah how good God is
To suffer us be born just now, when youth
That else would rust, can slake his blade in gore
Where very God Himself does seem to walk
The bloody fields of Flanders He so loves.

Arthur Graeme West

The Night Patrol

France, March 1916

Over the top! The wire's thin here, unbarbed
Plain rusty coils, not staked, and low enough:
Full of old tins, though – 'When you're through, all
    three,
Aim quarter left for fifty yards or so,
Then straight for that new piece of German wire;
See if it's thick, and listen for a while
For sounds of working; don't run any risks;
About an hour; now, over!'
                   And we placed
Our hands on the topmost sand-bags, leapt, and
    stood
A second with curved backs, then crept to the wire,
Wormed ourselves tinkling through, glanced back,
    and dropped.
The sodden ground was splashed with shallow pools,
And tufts of crackling cornstalks, two years old,
No man had reaped, and patches of spring grass.
Half-seen, as rose and sank the flares, were strewn
With the wrecks of our attack: the bandoliers.
Packs, rifles, bayonets, belts, and haversacks,
Shell fragments, and the huge whole forms of shells
Shot fruitlessly – and everywhere the dead.
Only the dead were always present – present
As a vile sickly smell of rottenness;
The rustling stubble and the early grass,
The slimy pools – the dead men stank through all,

Pungent and sharp: as bodies loomed before,
And as we passed they stank: then dulled away
To what vague foetor, all encompassing,
Infecting earth and air. They lay, all clothed,
Each in some new and piteous attitude
That we well marked to guide us back: as he,
Outside our wire, that lay on his back and crossed
His legs Crusader-wise; I smiled at that,
And thought on Elia and his Temple Church.
From him, at quarter-left, lay a small corpse,
Down in a hollow, huddled as in bed,
That one of us put his hand on unawares.
Next was a bunch of half a dozen men
All blown to bits, an archipelago
Of corrupt fragments, vexing to us three,
Who had no light to see by, save the flares.
On such a trail, so lit, for ninety yards
We crawled on belly and elbows, till we saw,
Instead of lumpish dead before our eyes,
The stakes and crosslines of the German wire.
We lay in shelter of the last dead man,
Ourselves as dead, and heard their shovels ring
Turning the earth, then talk and cough at times.
A sentry fired and a machine-gun spat;
They shot a flare above us, when it fell
And spluttered out in the pools of No Man's Land,
We turned and crawled past the remembered dead:
Past him and him, and them and him, until,
For he lay some way apart, we caught the scent
Of the Crusader and slid past his legs,
And through the wire and home, and got our rum.

Cameron Wilson

A Soldier

He laughed. His blue eyes searched the morning,
Found the unceasing song of the lark
In a brown twinkle of wings, far out.
Great clouds, like galleons, sailed the distance.
The young spring day had slipped the cloak of dark
And stood up straight and naked with a shout.
Through the green wheat, like laughing schoolboys,
Tumbled the yellow mustard flowers, uncheck'd.
The wet earth reeked and smoked in the sun …
He thought of the waking farm in England
The deep thatch of the roof – all shadow-fleck'd
The clank of pails at the pump … the day begun.
'After the war …' he thought. His heart beat faster
With a new love for things familiar and plain.
The Spring leaned down and whispered to him low
Of a slim, brown-throated woman he had kissed …
He saw, in sons that were himself again,
The only immortality that man may know.

And then a sound grew out of the morning,
And a shell came, moving a destined way,
Thin and swift and lustful, making its moan.
A moment his brave white body knew the Spring,
The next, it lay
In a red ruin of blood and guts and bone.

*   *   *

Oh! nothing was tortured there! Nothing could
    know
How death blasphemed all men and their high birth
With his obscenities. Already moved,
Within those shattered tissues, that dim force,
Which is the ancient alchemy of Earth,
Changing him to the very flowers he loved.

    *   *   *

'Nothing was tortured there!' Oh, pretty thought!
When God Himself might well bow down His head
And hide His haunted eyes before the dead.

Cameron Wilson

Magpies in Picardy

The magpies in Picardy
Are more than I can tell.
They flicker down the dusty roads
And cast a magic spell
On the men who march through Picardy,
Through Picardy to hell.

(The blackbird flies with panic,
The swallow goes like light,
The finches move like ladies,
The owl floats by at night;
But the great and flashing magpie
He flies as artists might.)

A magpie in Picardy
Told me secret things –
Of the music in white feathers,
And the sunlight that sings
And dances in deep shadows –
He told me with his wings.

(The hawk is cruel and rigid,
He watches from a height;
The rook is slow and sombre,
The robin loves to fight;
But the great and flashing magpie
He flies as lovers might.)

He told me that in Picardy,
An age ago or more,
While all his fathers still were eggs,
These dusty highways bore
Brown, singing soldiers marching out
Through Picardy to war.

He said that still through chaos
Works on the ancient plan,
And two things have altered not
Since first the world began –
The beauty of the wild green earth
And the bravery of man.

(For the sparrow flies unthinking
And quarrels in his flight.
The heron trails his legs behind,
The lark goes out of sight;
But the great and flashing magpie
He flies as poets might.)

Cameron Wilson

Song of Amiens

Lord! How we laughed in Amiens!
For here were lights, and good French drink,
And Marie smiled at everyone,
And Madeleine's new blouse was pink,
And Petite Jeanne (who always runs)
Served us so charmingly, I think
That we forgot the unsleeping guns.

Lord! How we laughed in Amiens!
Till through the talk there flashed the name
Of some great man we left behind.
And then a sudden silence came
And even Petite Jeanne (who runs)
Stood still to hear, with eyes aflame,
The distant mutter of the guns.

Ah! How we laughed in Amiens!
For there were useless things to buy,
Simply because Irene, who served,
Had happy laughter in her eye;
And Yvonne, bringing sticky buns,
Cared nothing that the eastern sky
Was lit with flashes from the guns.

And still we laughed in Amiens,
As dead men laughed a week ago.
What cared we if in Delville Wood
The splintered trees saw hell below?
We cared … We cared … But laughter runs
The cleanest stream a man may know
To rinse him from the taint of guns.

Cameron Wilson

Sportsmen in Paradise

They left the fury of the fight,
And they were very tired.
The gates of Heaven were open, quite
Unguarded, and unwired.
There was no sound of any gun;
The land was still and green:
Wide hills lay silent in the sun,
Blue valleys slept between.

They saw far off a little wood
Stand up against the sky.
Knee-deep in grass a great tree stood …
Some lazy cows went by …
There were some rooks sailed overhead –
And once a church-bell pealed.
'God! but it's England,' someone said,
'And there's a cricket field!'

Cyril Winterbotham

O.C. Platoon Enquiries

I once had a lovely platoon, Sir,
The finest platoon ever seen,
They could drill 'neath the sun, or the moon, Sir,
They were fit, and their rifles were clean.

They could march, and they knew how to shoot, Sir,
And to bayonet sacks upon sticks,
Equipped from the cap to the boot, Sir,
– Their number was fifty and six.

They were infantry right to the core, Sir,
They trusted in bullets and steel
To finish the terrible war, Sir,
– It bucked them all up a good deal.

But as soon as we landed in France, Sir,
Such terrible changes began
That hardly a man had a chance, Sir,
Of being an Infantry man.

For some for the transport have left, Sir
And one cuts up beef for the Staff,
And others, of whom I'm bereft, Sir,
Mend trousers that suffer from 'STRAFE.'

There are some who are Sanit'ry men, Sir,
– (We tread upon dubious paths) –
And some became sappers, and then, Sir,
They lived among boilers and baths.

The M.G.O. pinched a few more, Sir,
– And blood-thirsty beggars they be –
They're especially out for the gore, Sir,
Of Huns that are carrying Tea.

One's running a photograph show, Sir,
Another is making a map,
There are servants and grooms, one or two, Sir,
They all leave a bit of a gap.

There are some who are Officers now, Sir,
While others wield clippers and shave,
There are bandsmen all under a vow, Sir,
To hearten the steps of the brave.

The few that remain use the bomb, Sir,
Proficient in anarchist lore
They handle H.E. with aplomb, Sir,
I look on with obvious awe.

If my men are all details am I, Sir,
A detail myself! and if so,
Am I O.C. Platoon still, and why, Sir,
Is what I should just like to know.

W.B. Yeats

An Irish Airman Foresees His Death

I know that I shall meet my fate
Somewhere among the clouds above;
Those that I fight I do not hate,
Those that I guard I do not love;
My country is Kiltartan Cross,
My countrymen Kiltartan's poor,
No likely end could bring them loss
Or leave them happier than before.
Nor law, nor duty bade me fight,
Nor public men, nor cheering crowds,
A lonely impulse of delight
Drove to this tumult in the clouds;
I balanced all, brought all to mind,
The years to come seemed waste of breath,
A waste of breath the years behind
In balance with this life, this death.

W.B. Yeats

On Being Asked for a War Poem

I think it better that in times like these
A poet's mouth should be silent, for in truth
We have no gift to set a statesman right;
He has had enough of meddling who can please
A young girl in the indolence of her youth,
Or an old man upon a winter's night.

BIOGRAPHIES

Raymond Asquith (1879–1916)
Born in 1878, the son of H.H. Asquith, who was to become Prime Minister from 1908 to 1916. Raymond Asquith was a Fellow of All Souls' College, Oxford and a barrister. He was killed in an attack near Ginchy on 15 September 1916, at the Battle of Flers-Courcelette.

Maurice Baring (1874–1945)
A younger son of Lord Revelstoke, Baring joined the diplomatic service. During the war he worked in Intelligence and was attached to the Royal Flying Corps. After the war he had a career as a dramatist, novelist and critic.

R.H. Beckh (1894–1916)
Beckh planned to take Holy Orders and do missionary work in India if he survived the war. He was killed near Robecq.

William Eric Berridge (1894–1916)
Berridge was educated at Eton and New College Oxford and joined the Somerset Light Infantry in December 1914. He died of wounds near Arras.

Laurence Binyon (1869–1943)
A Quaker, Binyon worked in hospitals in France during the war. Most of his life was spent at The British Museum, where he became Keeper of Prints and Drawings.

John Peele Bishop (1892–1944)
Born in Virginia and educated at Princeton, Bishop served in France with the US 33rd Infantry. He was a man of letters and is thought to be the model for character Thomas Parke D'Invilliers in F. Scott Fitzgerald's first novel, *This Side of Paradise*.

Walter Charles Blackall (1876–1918)
Blackall was a professional soldier and served with The

Buffs in the Second Boer War. By December 1917 he was commanding 4th Battalion South Staffordshire Regiment. He was killed near Bapaume.

Edmund Blunden (1896–1974)

Poet, critic and teacher, Blunden served as an infantryman almost throughout the war and was awarded the Military Cross. Perhaps best known for his prose account *Undertones of War*, he succeeded Robert Graves as Professor of Poetry at Oxford.

Rupert Brooke (1887–1915)

Brooke enjoyed a brilliant career as an undergraduate at King's College, Cambridge, where he was elected into a Fellowship. He was commissioned in the Royal Naval Division in 1914, and took part in the Siege of Antwerp. He died of blood-poisoning en route to Gallipoli.

Edward Carpenter (1844–1929)

Carpenter was an English socialist poet, socialist philosopher, anthologist, and early gay activist. *Lieutenant Tattoon, M.C.* is a thinly veiled commentary on Siegfried Sassoon's protest against the war.

G.K. Chesterton (1874–1936)

Essayist, novelist, poet and Catholic apologist, Chesterton was a witty, energetic and mostly facile poet, probably best known for his Father Brown detective stories.

Margaret Postgate Cole (1893–1980)

Cole was a classics teacher and a Fabian, who worked for the Labour Research Department. The sister of Raymond Postgate, she was married to G.D.H. Cole.

Leslie Coulson (1889–1916)

Coulson was a well-known journalist before the war. He enlisted as a Private in 2nd Battalion the London Regiment of the Royal Fusiliers, was wounded at Gallipoli and died of wounds during the Battle of Le Transloy on the Somme.

Jeffrey Day (1896–1918)

Born in St Ives, Day joined the Royal Naval Air Service and rose to the rank of Flight Commander. He was shot down at sea whilst engaging six enemy aircraft.

Alec de Candole (1897–1918)

De Candole was a near contemporary and friend of C.H. Sorley at Marlborough College. He won a scholarship to Trinity College Cambridge in 1915 and enlisted in April 1916. He was killed in a bombing raid near Arras.

Oliphant Down (1886–1917)

Captain Down of 4th Battalion Royal Berkshire Regiment was awarded the MC in 1916. He was killed near Cambrai in May 1917.

F.S. Flint (1885–1960)

Frank Stuart Flint was a poet, translator and Civil Servant. Prominent among the Imagists he was a friend of Ezra Pound and T.E. Hulme.

Clifford Flower (1891–1917)

After leaving school at thirteen, Flower became a draughtsman in the iron and steel industry. He volunteered in 1914, but was rejected for being below regulation height, but enlisted with the personal intervention of Lord Kitchener. He was killed in April 1917.

Gilbert Frankau (1884–1952)

Frankau served in the East Surrey Regiment and the Royal Artillery. He fought at Loos, Ypres and the Somme, and was invalided out in 1918. He was a poet, novelist, short story writer and cigar importer.

H.R. Freston (1891–1916)

Rex Freston was reading English at Exeter College, Oxford before being commissioned into the 6th Battalion Royal Berkshire Regiment in 1915. He was killed by a shell in January 1916 near La Boiselle.

Crosbie Garstin (1887–1930)

Garstin travelled the world in a variety of jobs such as cowboy, miner, bouncer and lumberjack but enlisted in 1914. Born in Cornwall he became famous after the war for his *Penhale* trilogy.

Wilfred Gibson (1878–1962)

A close friend of Rupert Brooke's, Gibson became a social worker. He published several volumes of poetry and his war poems celebrated the private soldier.

Robert Graves (1895–1985)

Graves served in France in the Royal Welch Fusiliers and was a friend of Siegfried Sassoon. Famous for his autobiographical *Goodbye to All That*, *I, Claudius* and *The White Goddess*, he was Professor of Poetry at Oxford from 1961 to 1966.

Julian Grenfell (1888–1915)

Best remembered for 'Into Battle', Grenfell was a professional soldier in the Royal Dragoons. He died of wounds on 30 April 1915.

Ivor Gurney (1890–1937)

Gurney was a brilliant musician who joined the 2/5th Battalion of the Gloucester Regiment in 1915. He saw service on the Western Front from June 1916 until he was invalided home in September 1917 after being gassed in the Passchendaele offensive. He never fully recovered from the war and died of tuberculosis.

Thomas Hardy (1840–1928)
An architect and novelist, Hardy forswore novels after the hostile reception to *Jude the Obscure*, and concentrated on his poetry. He was awarded the Order of Merit in 1910.

J.H.M. Hardyman (1894–1918)
The distinguished zoologist Hardyman enlisted in August 1914. Between April 1917 and May 1918 he was promoted from Lieutenant to Lieutenant-Colonel, and was killed during the Battle of Albert.

A.P. Herbert (1890–1971)
Barrister, humorist, novelist, playwright and law reform activist. He was an independent Member of Parliament for the University of Oxford. His novel, *The Secret Battle*, is a telling indictment of the war.

John Hobson (1893–1917)
A history scholar of Christ Church, Oxford, Hobson was commissioned in September 1914 in the Royal Scots. He commanded a section of the 116th Machine Gun Company and was killed by a shell near Ypres in July 1917.

William Noel Hodgson (1893–1916)
'Smiler' Hodgson MC was the son of the first Bishop of St Edmundsbury and Ipswich. A classical scholar of Christ Church, Oxford, he was killed on the first day of the Battle of the Somme near Mametz.

A.E. Housman (1859–1936)
Professor of Latin first at London University then at Cambridge, Housman is most famous for *A Shropshire Lad*, but his mordant temperament was ideally suited to the tragedy of the Great War.

T.E. Hulme (1883–1917)
Something of a hell-raiser, Hulme was sent down from Cambridge. He became a dominant figure in London's literary life and formed the Poets' Club. He enlisted as a

Private in the Honourable Artillery Company in 1914, was commissioned in the Royal Marine Artillery in 1916 and killed by shellfire near Nieupoort.

Philip Johnstone (1890–1968)

John Stanley Purvis, who wrote under the pseudonym of Philip Johnstone, was invalided out of the army after been wounded during the Battle of the Somme and returned to Cranleigh School in Surrey where he had previously taught. He became Canon Purvis of York, and internationally famous for his versions of the York mystery plays.

G.A. Studdert Kennedy (1883–1929)

Leeds-born Kennedy was an Anglican clergyman who joined the Army Chaplain's Department in 1915 and was awarded the MC in 1917. He served mostly behind the lines, but had three spells in the trenches.

Rudyard Kipling (1865–1936)

Widely regarded as the poet of Empire and Nobel prizewinner for literature in 1907, Kipling's work took on a darker tone after the death of his 18-year-old son John (Jack) at the Battle of Loos in 1915.

Winifred M. Letts (1882–1972)

Letts spent much of her life in Ireland. Her early work was for the Abbey Theatre in Dublin, and she wrote several novels and children's books as well as *Knockmaroon*, an account of her childhood in Dublin.

W.S.S. Lyon (1886–1915)

As a Lieutenant in the Territorial Army, Lyon was called up in August 1914; he was killed at the Second Battle of Ypres in May 1915. *Easter at Ypres and Other Poems* was published in 1916.

E.A. Mackintosh (1893–1917)
Mackintosh left his studies at Christ Church, Oxford to join the 5th Seaforth Highlanders. He was wounded on the Somme in 1916 and killed at Cambrai in October 1917.

John McCrae (1872–1918)
'In Flanders Fields' appeared in *Punch* in December 1915; its author was a Canadian doctor who had enlisted as a gunner, but who transferred to the Medical Services. He had just been appointed consultant to all the British Armies in France when he died of pneumonia.

A.J. Mann (1896–1917)
Second Lieutenant Mann served in the 8th Battalion, The Black Watch and his poems show the fatalism which affected so many soldiers. He died of wounds during the Battle of Arras.

Frederick Manning (1882–1925)
Sydney-born Manning settled in England in 1903. He joined the Shropshire Light Infantry and served on the Somme. His 1929 novel, *The Middle Parts of Fortune* gives a graphic account of life at the front; an expurgated edition was published as *Her Privates We* in 1930.

John Masefield (1878–1967)
Famous for his 1911 narrative poem 'The Everlasting Mercy', shocking in its realism, Masefield served as a Red Cross orderly in France and commanded a motor-boat ambulance service at Gallipoli. He was appointed Poet Laureate in 1930.

Charlotte Mew (1869–1928)
'The Cenotaph' comes from *The Farmer's Bride*, published by Harold Monro's Poetry Bookshop. Mew suffered from ill-health all her life and, despite patronage by Thomas Hardy and others, committed suicide by drinking disinfectant.

Vincent Morris (1896–1917)

Morris's *The Eleventh Hour* was written in frustration when he was too young to enlist. He joined the Sherwood Foresters but transferred to the Royal Flying Corps and died of wounds in April 1917.

Sir Henry Newbolt (1862–1938)

Newbolt is best known for 'Vitaï Lampada' (There's a breathless hush in the Close tonight) and 'Drake's Drum' but the contrasting poems in this anthology give some clue to his many-sided character.

Robert Nichols (1893–1944)

Nichols was in the Royal Artillery but was invalided home in 1916 with shell-shock. He was a friend of Brooke and Sassoon and preceded Edmund Blunden as Professor of English Literature at the University of Tokyo.

Wilfred Owen (1893–1918)

Owen was serving in the Manchester Regiment when he was invalided home after six months at the Front in 1917 and sent to Craiglockhart Hospital in Edinburgh where he met Siegfried Sassoon. Sassoon encouraged his poetry, and he wrote an astonishing body of poems between then and his death, seven days before the Armistice.

Robert Palmer (1888–1916)

The second son of Lord Selborne, Robert Palmer had a great future ahead of him as a lawyer. He joined the Royal Hampshire Regiment in 1914 and was killed in Mesopotamia in 1916.

Harold Parry (1896–1917)

Parry went to Exeter College, Oxford in 1915 as an Open History Scholar but enlisted in January 1916. Few of his poems mention the war directly. He was killed by shellfire near Ypres on 6 May 1917.

Vivian Pemberton (1894–1918)

Pemberton enlisted into the Royal Munster Fusiliers in 1914 and was transferred to the Royal Garrison Artillery. He won a Military Cross in 1918 and was killed in action at Sancourt, near Cambrai.

Max Plowman (1883–1941)

Commissioned in the West Yorkshire Regiment, Plowman was a reluctant soldier. He fought on the Somme, spent time in Craiglockhart Hospital, resigned his commission and was court-martialed for desertion and wrote the moving *A Subaltern on the Somme*. He became Secretary of the Peace Pledge Union.

Jessie Pope (1868–1941)

Pope was a writer of satirical fiction and verse for popular magazines. Her patriotic poems contrast with those of Owen, Sassoon and other war poets, but she achieved some sort of redemption by effecting the publication of *The Ragged Trousered Philanthropists*.

Edgell Rickword (1898–1982)

From school, Rickword joined the Artists' Rifles, was commissioned in 1917 and awarded the Military Cross. After the war he became an influential literary critic as well as being an active poet, and edited the *Left Review*.

Isaac Rosenberg (1890–1918)

Rosenberg was the son of Jewish immigrants. He studied at the Slade School of Arts and was taken up by Laurence Binyon and Edward Marsh. He enlisted in 1915. He served on the Western Front though totally unsuited to it by health, short stature and disposition. He was killed on 1 April. He is widely regarded as one of the great poets of the First World War.

Siegfried Sassoon (1886–1967)

Sassoon was educated at Marlborough College and Cambridge. He enlisted on the outbreak of war and served on the Western Front, being wounded and awarded the Military Cross. His public protest about the conduct of the war led to his hospitalisation at Craiglockhart, where he met Wilfred Owen. *Memoirs of an Infantry Officer* is his account of the war.

Alan Seeger (1888–1916)

The American Seeger was a contemporary of T.S. Eliot at Harvard and enlisted in the French Foreign Legion in August 1914. He fought in Champagne and on the Somme, where he was killed by machine-gun fire on 4th July 1916.

Patrick Shaw-Stuart (1888–1917)

Considered as having one of the most brilliant minds of his generation, Shaw-Stuart was in the Royal Naval Division, and with Brooke at his death. He served at Gallipoli and the Western Front, and was killed near Cambrai on 30 December 1917.

Osbert Sitwell (1892–1969)

Sitwell joined the Grenadier Guards in 1912. He fought on the Western Front at Loos, but blood-poisoning in 1916 curtailed his military career. His post-war writing was prolific, principally criticism, novels and poetry. His sister was Edith Sitwell.

Hugh Smith (1889–1916)

Smith resigned his post as District Commissioner in Nigeria to join the Argyll and Sutherland Highlanders. He was killed in an attack on High Wood on the Somme on 18 August 1916.

Charles Hamilton Sorley (1895–1915)

Sorley was educated at Marlborough College, and was a Scholar at University College, Oxford when he enlisted in the Suffolk Regiment in 1914. He was posted to France in May 1915 and was killed at the Battle of Loos on 13 October. Robert Graves described him as being one of the three poets of importance killed in the war, the other two being Owen and Rosenberg.

J.C. Squire (1884–1958)

Squire was a successful poet, parodist, essayist and anthologiser. He was literary editor, then acting editor of the *New Statesman*, and founded the *London Mercury*.

J.E. Stewart (1889–1918)

A former teacher, Stewart enlisted in August 1914 and was commissioned into the Border Regiment two months later. He was wounded, awarded the MC and promoted to Lieut. Colonel in the South Staffordshire Regiment. He was killed in the fighting for Mount Kemmel on 26 April 1918.

Edward Wyndham Tennant (1897–1916)

Tennant enlisted in the Grenadier Guards in August 1914. He was sent to France the following year and shared a dugout with Osbert Sitwell. He was killed in September 1916 on the Somme and is buried close to his friend Raymond Asquith.

Edward Thomas (1878–1917)

Educated at St Paul's School and Lincoln College, Oxford, Thomas was a professional writer of travel books and histories, reviews and essays. Under the influence of his friend Robert Frost he started to write poetry in 1914. He enlisted in 1915 and was killed by the passage of a shell during the Battle of Arras in 1917.

R.E. Vernède (1875–1917)

Vernède was a poet, novelist and short story writer when he enlisted in 1914, four years over the age-limit. He was wounded during the Battle of the Somme, refused a War Office posting, and was killed near Cambrai.

Gilbert Waterhouse (1883–1916)

Waterhouse was an architect who enlisted in September 1914. He was commissioned into the Essex Regiment in April 1915. He was killed on the first day of the Battle of the Somme, 1 July 1916. *The Rail-Head and Other Poems* was published posthumously in December 1916.

Arthur Graeme West (1891–1917)

Initially rejected because of poor eyesight, West became a Private in the Public Schools Battalion in 1915. Posted to France in November, he was commissioned in 1916 and returned to France where he was killed by a sniper's bullet in April 1917.

T.P. Cameron Wilson (1889–1918)

Wilson was a young schoolmaster who had written two novels and some poetry when he enlisted in August 1914. He was commissioned into the Sherwood Foresters and rose to the rank of Captain. He was killed in action in the Somme valley on 23 March 1918.

Cyril Winterbotham (1887–1916)

Winterbotham was a barrister who stood for Parliament in 1913. He was commissioned in the Gloucestershire Regiment in October 1914 and served in France between March 1915 and August 1916. He was killed on the Somme on 14 August 1916.

W.B. Yeats (1865–1939)

Yeats was the greatest Anglo-Irish poet of his time. The Irish Rising in 1916 moved him more than did the First World War, and he assumed the role of leader of the Irish literary renaissance. He was awarded the Nobel Prize in Literature in 1923.

INDEX OF FIRST LINES

ACKNOWLEDGEMENTS

For permission to reprint copyright material, the publishers gratefully acknowledge the following:

A.P. Watt at United Agents on behalf of The Trustees of the Maurice Baring Will Trust for 'August 1914'.

David Higham on behalf of the Estate of Edmund Blunden for 'The Zonnebeke Road' and '1916 Seen From 1921' from *Selected Poems* published by Carcanet Press Ltd.

David Higham on behalf of the Estate of Margaret Cole for 'The Veteran'.

A.P. Watt at United Agents on behalf of Timothy D'Arch Smith for Gilbert Frankau's 'The Deserter'.

Linda and Oliver Flint for 'Lament' by F.S. Flint.

Carcanet Press Ltd 'A Dead Boche' and 'The Last Post' from *Complete Poems in One Volume* by Robert Graves.

A.P. Watt at United Agents on behalf of the executors of the Estate of Jocelyn Herbert, M.T. Perkins and Polly M.V.R. Perkins for 'Beaucourt Revisited' by A.P. Herbert.

The following poems by Siegfried Sassoon: 'Aftermath', 'Attack', 'Base Details', 'Counter-Attack', 'Died of Wounds', 'Does It Matter?' 'Glory of Women', 'On Passing the New Menin Gate', 'The General', 'The Hero', 'They', 'To Any Dead Officer', 'To One Who Was With Me', 'Trench Duty', 'Wirers' are all Copyright Siegfried Sassoon by kind permission of the Estate of George Sassoon.

David Higham on behalf of the Estate of Osbert Sitwell for 'Armchair'.

Roger Squire for 'The Dilemma' by J.C. Squire from *The Survival of the Fittest* published in 1916.

In this anthology, the publishers have made every effort to trace the copyright holders of all poems in copyright. They would be interested to hear from any copyright holders not here acknowledged.